Globalization in a Glass

Food in Modern History: Traditions and Innovations

Series Editors
Peter Scholliers
Amy Bentley

This new monograph series pays serious attention to food as a focal point in historical events from the late eighteenth century to present day. Employing the lens of technology broadly construed, the series highlights the nutritional, social, political, cultural, and economic transformations of food around the globe. It features new scholarship that considers ever-intensifying and accelerating tensions between tradition and innovation that characterize the modern era. The editors are particularly committed to publishing manuscripts featuring geographical areas currently underrepresented in English-language academic publications, including the Global South, particularly Africa and Asia, as well as monographs featuring indigenous and under-represented groups, and non-western societies.

Published

Food and Aviation in the Twentieth Century: The Pan American Ideal,
Bryce Evans (2021)
Feeding the People in Wartime Britain,
Bryce Evans (2022)
Rebellious Cooks and Recipe Writing in Communist Bulgaria,
Albena Shkodrova (2022)

Globalization in a Glass

The Rise of Pilsner Beer through Technology, Taste and Empire

Malcolm F. Purinton

BLOOMSBURY ACADEMIC
LONDON • NEW YORK • OXFORD • NEW DELHI • SYDNEY

BLOOMSBURY ACADEMIC
Bloomsbury Publishing Plc
50 Bedford Square, London, WC1B 3DP, UK
1385 Broadway, New York, NY 10018, USA
29 Earlsfort Terrace, Dublin 2, Ireland

BLOOMSBURY, BLOOMSBURY ACADEMIC and the Diana logo are
trademarks of Bloomsbury Publishing Plc

First published in Great Britain 2023
This paperback edition published 2024

Copyright © Malcolm F. Purinton, 2023

Malcolm F. Purinton has asserted his right under the Copyright,
Designs and Patents Act, 1988, to be identified as Author of this work.

For legal purposes the Acknowledgments on pp. vii–viii constitute an
extension of this copyright page.

Cover image © The manufacture of wooden beer barrels in Pilsen, 1880s.
From the collection of Plzensky Prazdroj Museum. Photo by Fine Art
Images/Heritage Images/Getty Images.

All rights reserved. No part of this publication may be reproduced or transmitted
in any form or by any means, electronic or mechanical, including photocopying,
recording, or any information storage or retrieval system, without prior
permission in writing from the publishers.

Bloomsbury Publishing Plc does not have any control over, or responsibility for,
any third-party websites referred to or in this book. All internet addresses given
in this book were correct at the time of going to press. The author and publisher
regret any inconvenience caused if addresses have changed or sites have
ceased to exist, but can accept no responsibility for any such changes.

A catalogue record for this book is available from the British Library.

A catalog record for this book is available from the Library of Congress.

ISBN:	HB:	978-1-3503-2437-4
	PB:	978-1-3503-2785-6
	ePDF:	978-1-3503-2438-1
	eBook:	978-1-3503-2439-8

Series: Food in Modern History: Traditions and Innovations

Typeset by Integra Software Services Pvt. Ltd.

To find out more about our authors and books visit www.bloomsbury.com
and sign up for our newsletters.

Contents

List of Illustrations vi
Acknowledgments vii

Introduction: The Taste of Modernity 1
1 Ales for Everyone: English and Continental Brewing Industries, 1750–1870 13
2 Modern Methods: European Brewing Technology and Science 49
3 Making the Investments Count: Business Strategies of Brewing Industries 73
4 Where the Beer Flowed: Migrations and Markets 99
5 Where the Beer Flowed: British Imperial Trade Networks 121
6 It Tasted Better: Why the People Chose the Pilsner 139
Conclusion 165

Bibliography 168
Index 175

List of Illustrations

1.1	London Porter Brewery	23
1.2	A Brewhouse Yard	28
2.1	Pilsen Brewhouse	55
2.2	Schwechat Brewery Vienna	57
2.3	Carlsberg Laboratory	69
3.1	J. C. Jacobsen, Carlsberg Brewery, 1886	80
3.2	Spaten Brewery, Late Nineteenth Century	82
4.1	Engel & Wolf's Brewery and Vaults, Philadelphia, USA	106
5.1	Carlton Brewery—Melbourne Australia	135

Acknowledgments

This project has benefited from the kind support of many colleagues, friends, and family over the many years since it began as a vague collection of ideas and hypotheses. From the early graduate school years of discussion in the now-closed Boston dive bar of Punters to many couches surfed while visiting archives across Europe, I have received an incredible amount of support from friends, friends of friends, and others and I thank them all for the support and consideration of my project. Long before these ideas began to take shape, my parents, Barbara and Charlie, have supported me in more ways than I can count and over more years than I'd like to admit. Without their continuous care and support of my goals, dreams, and adventures none of this would have been possible, I thank you both so very much. This book would not be what it is either without the love and patience from my wife, Jenni. She has been a source of constant support and compassion throughout this long process that began many years ago before we even knew each other. Her encouragement and understanding during the recent years of full teaching-loads, moves, and a pandemic alongside ongoing research and writing to put this project, and all its many parts, together, have been an important part of how it has come to fruition.

More than anyone, Professor Heather Street-Salter has given far more of her time and attention to this project and to my career than should be expected from any advisor or mentor. From a chance meeting at my first World History Association conference in Salem, MA to bringing me across the country twice in a single year for my doctoral degree work she has always had my best interests at heart. From all the conversations across time zones for many years to helping with the final drafts of this manuscript, she has been patient and supportive through all the turns my life has taken and I can never thank her enough for everything, especially for always being certain about me even when I had my doubts. I hope this book stands as a humble tribute to her guidance and hard work.

I also must thank Northeastern University and especially the History Department for their support as well. To Kate Luongo who first suggested that I write about empire and beer all those years ago, I had no idea this is where that literature review suggestion about imperial alcohol policies in Africa would take me, so thank you. Bonnie Knipfer and Kirsten Bilas worked as the stellar admin team for the department for most of my time as a graduate student, and then as a professor, with regular fun conversations and the answers to all my questions they made the daily life of the department much more enjoyable and were the engine that kept everything working, for everyone.

Without the people who shared their homes and their time this process would have been much less fun and much more stressful. Sally Walkerman and Nick Calvery opened their English home to me several times over the years and provided much needed conversations and decompression after long days in libraries and archives. Friends and colleagues from the World History Association have always been sources of constant support as well. Others who kept me going and laughing include Shawna Herzog, Alex Davis, Matt Pyle, James Bradford, Dave Decamp, Olivier Schouteden, Sarah Peck, and of course Allyssa Metzger. Thank you all! And also, one of my key mentors and supporters from my dissertation committee, Professor Trevor Getz continues to be an inspiration with his incredible ongoing work.

At the beginning of this project, I was not actually a fan of pilsner myself. The incongruities of the history of this first golden lager with the British Empire just drew me in and led me on adventures that have helped change my perspective of the world and its history with such an ancient substance as beer. I have since grown very fond of the pilsner and all of the myriad golden lagers that have come out of the original 1842 creation in the city of Pilsen. One of my favorite memories that helped me appreciate this style of beer on a more tangible and personal level was when the founder of the Burlington, Vermont-based Zero Gravity Brewery, Paul Sayler took the time to tell me his story of why he brewed the Green State Lager at a moment when I needed to reconnect with the more physical, and delicious, aspects of my topic. Paul solidified for me the sincere complexity and difficulty of producing an excellent light golden lager. Sometimes the seemingly simplest of ingredients and production demand the most attention and skill, something that is especially true in this case. Thank you, Paul, for the pints of perspective right when I needed them.

Introduction: The Taste of Modernity

In 1885, the British *Brewer's Journal* exclaimed, "Nothing more strikingly exemplifies the wide influence of England all over the world than the way in which our national beverage, beer, finds its way to all quarters of the globe."[1] This boast, however, proved short-lived: within fifteen years, consumers worldwide had turned overwhelmingly to drinking Continental pilsner beer. Pilsner-style beer, light golden-colored lagers, represented 84 percent of the world beer market in 2020, up from three-quarters of all beer consumed and produced in the world in 2013 when the top four pilsner-style brewers—Anheuser-Bush InBev (AB InBev), SABMiller, Heineken, and Carlsberg—accounted for over half the global market for beer.[2] With the 2016 merger between AB InBev and SABMiller, the company produces more than double its nearest competitor by volume, Heineken.[3]

Much has been written about beer and the history of brewing, but most of these works have been—and continue to be—uncritical popular accounts rather than academic histories. Moreover, most of what has been written has focused on national or local traditions in the United States and the UK

---

[1] "Interesting Facts," *Brewers' Journal*, 1/15/1885.
[2] The Business Research Company, "Update: Beer Global Market Report 2021 Including Market Size, Share & Growth Analysis, Global Beer Consumption Statistics," April 1, 2021, https://www.globenewswire.com/en/news-release/2021/04/01/2203506/0/en/Update-Beer-Global-Market-Report-2021-Including-Market-Size-Share-Growth-Analysis-Global-Beer-Consumption-Statistics.html, accessed October 11, 2022; David Jones, "Top Four Brewers Account for over Half of World's Beer," *Reuters*, February 10, 2010, http://www.reuters.com/article/2010/02/08/beer-idUSLDE61723K20100208, accessed January 30, 2013.
[3] Ketih Gribbins, "The 40 Biggest Breweries in the World in 2021," in *Craft Brewing Business*, June 13, 2022, https://www.craftbrewingbusiness.com/business-marketing/the-40-biggest-breweries-in-the-world-in-2021/, accessed October 11, 2022.

and has disregarded larger global trends and connections.[4] These laudatory accounts have spilled over into television, as in the Discovery Channel's 2011 production of *How Beer Saved the World*. This documentary combined cartoons and snippets of interviews with academics and popular writers to promote the value of beer as being the reason for everything from the founding of human civilization, to the building of the Egyptian pyramids, to the development of germ theory.[5] Even the *Oxford Companion to Beer*, which includes over 1,100 entries, was edited by a brewer and includes contributors who lack academic training and do little more than repeat old myths and stories.[6] Indeed, the persistence of beer myths and legends supported by beer writers and journalists serves as a potent reminder of the need for critical scholarship of this important commodity.

In the past four decades the surge of smaller independent craft breweries, first in the United States and now growing across the world, has created a credible threat to the large industrial macro-breweries that have held sway over the global beer markets for over a century. One of the most important aspects of these smaller breweries is that the styles of beer they generally produce set themselves self-consciously apart from the larger macro-breweries. Craft breweries almost entirely concentrate on producing beer styles reminiscent of those produced in the UK between the late eighteenth century and the middle of the nineteenth century following the industrialization of the British brewing industry. Craft breweries produce these British ale styles including pale ales, stouts, porters, and the wildly popular India Pale Ales as a stylistic rejection of the golden lagers of the world's largest brewing companies. These smaller, usually independently owned breweries market themselves against the much older, larger, and wealthier breweries by promoting themselves as being more careful with their brewing processes and more innovative in their use of

---

[4] To name only a few published with academic audiences in mind, see Peter Mathias, *The Brewing Industry in England, 1700-1830* (Cambridge [England]: Cambridge University Press, 1959); T. R. Gourvish and R. G. Wilson, *The British Brewing Industry, 1830-1980* (Cambridge [England]; New York: Cambridge University Press, 1994); Mikuláš Teich, *Bier, Wissenschaft und Wirtschaft in Deutschland 1800-1914: ein Beitrag zur deutschen Industrialisierungsgeschichte* (Wien: Böhlau, 2000); James Sumner, *Brewing Science, Technology and Print, 1700-1880* (Pittsburgh, PA: Pittsburgh University Press, 2016).

[5] Martyn Ives, *How Beer Saved the World* (Louisville, CO: Gaiam Americas, 2011).

[6] Garrett Oliver, *The Oxford Companion to Beer* (New York: Oxford University Press, 2012).

ingredients, which in turn allows them to produce beer with stronger flavors and, in many cases, higher alcohol content. Ironically, less than 150 years ago these same styles of beer were being pushed out of global beer markets precisely because of these characteristics in order to make room for the lighter and lower alcohol golden lagers.

The production of beer has been critical to health, consumption patterns, and trade in many areas around the world for millennia. However, until the nineteenth century beer production and trade were constrained to regional networks and limited imperial connections. Over the second half of the nineteenth century, beer quickly became a global commodity. Not only that, but one particular style of beer that had been limited to one specific region suddenly became the most widely traded and consumed beer in the world. Up until now, no one has examined in depth this sudden global domination of the pilsner-style beer.

This study is not only important as a study of beer as a commodity. Its greater importance is in the way the spread of the pilsner-style serves as a visible, traceable marker for the changes wrought by globalization in an age of empire. Its spread was dependent on not only technological innovations and faster transportation, but on the increased connectedness of the world including the political structures, such as empires, that dominated the world at the time.

The reasons for the spread of the pilsner, from which all the golden lager beers derive, over British beers are what interest me here. I argue that the rise to prominence of pilsners in the British colonies and elsewhere across the world was due to a unique combination of elements that were exploited successfully by Continental pilsner brewers to develop a consistent, high-quality product that reflected the changing tastes of beer consumers for a light-colored, low alcohol, highly carbonated beer. These include the development of new technologies for the brewing industry, decisions to use scientific methods in beer production, and business strategies regarding management and investment capital accumulation. Continental brewing companies used the latest science and technologies to develop and popularize pilsner beers as the style that most reflected progress and modernity in the late nineteenth century. Through these adoptions, the popularity of pilsner beer was able to spread far outside Europe, and Continental brewers soon gained control over export markets. This led to foreign markets copying the Continental pilsner-style and producing their own golden lagers for local consumption instead of choosing to produce British-style ales. In order to explain the ready acceptance of pilsner in foreign markets, I look at the migration of Germans to North and South America due to economics and political pressures in Europe from the 1830s to 1850s, the development of the Japanese beer brewing industry along German lines, and the British colonies in South Africa, British India, and Australia where European colonists chose to produce and consume Continental lager beer by the end of the nineteenth century instead of British beer styles. While empires are important in this study, I also argue that they must be viewed in their larger global context.[7] Without the inclusion of these broader connections, studies of colonialism and imperialism are missing vital information regarding how and why colonial consumers acted against their own nation's interests with their choices.

Quality of product is a key characteristic of taste used in the marketing of beer in the past (and the present) regardless of the style of beer, mode of production, or size of the brewing company. Today, craft breweries market their smaller size as proof of better quality (i.e. taste), arguing they can lavish more care on smaller batches of beer. In reality, however, craft breweries use the same technologies and scientific knowledge in their beer production as AB InBev does to produce its vast quantities of Budweiser. In the latter half of the nineteenth century, little overt marketing was needed to promote golden lagers produced in Germany and the rest of Continental Europe. The perceived high quality of golden lagers was instead promoted through ideas and notions of modernity and progress.

It is important to note that the general idea marking some beer styles as more "modern" than others was not new to the last half of the nineteenth century. However, it *was* novel to talk about Continental beer in such a way. Indeed, early industrial might placed the British brewing industry, and Ireland, at the apex of global beer manufacturing—both in terms of quantity and quality—from the mid-eighteenth to the mid-nineteenth centuries. Because Britain was the first nation to industrialize and use new technologies like steam power in

---

[7] See especially Heather Streets-Salter, *World War One in Southeast Asia: Colonialism and Anticolonialism in an Era of Global Conflict* (Cambridge: Cambridge University Press, 2017).

the brewing process, British brewers consistently produced the highest quality of beer, in the largest amounts, until around 1860. It was due to this reputation that Continental brewers sought out British technologies and utensils for their own use during the 1830s.[8]

Yet between 1870 and 1914, Continental beers, in the form of golden lagers, came to be understood as more modern than British "modern" beers. In this period, consumers came to believe that pilsner beers were inherently better, both in taste and for health, than British beer. Continental brewers seized the opportunity to push into new markets that were opening up through the development of global trade networks and European imperialism.[9]

The pilsner held several key attributes that made it appealing to a wide range of consumers. These attributes can all be included under the label of taste, including health benefits. As I detail in Chapter 7, taste played an essential role in the dissemination and acceptance of a singular global style of beer. The pilsner offered the consumer an item whose essence was wrapped in ideals of modern, rational thought via the inclusion of natural sciences in its very creation. Continental brewers were known for their early and rapid adoption of the latest scientific and technological breakthroughs in their brewing processes and within their breweries. In terms of taste, this appealed to consumers who sought an item that represented progress and a rational future inclusive of scientific and technological advance in comparison with traditional approaches and older styles of beer like those of the British.

In addition to the appeal of rationalization, the physical qualities of pilsner served as reminders of the purity of scientific innovation and the healthy qualities of the beer style. Through the adoption of science and technology, the brewers of pilsner were able to produce a consistent beer that was of a light and golden color with high levels of carbon dioxide and low percentages of alcohol. When consumers ordered a pilsner, they could be sure they would receive

---

[8] As discussed in Chapter 1 with the travels of Anton Dreher and Gabriel Sedlymayr Jr. in 1834.

[9] For example, Guinness stout was prescribed by doctors for decades due to its perceived health benefits. For more on how this affected Guinness overseas sale, see: Arthur Shand, "Report: MR. Shand's Journey through South Africa" (A. Guinness, Son & Co., Limited, St. James's Gate Brewery: Dublin, Ireland, 1904). Pilsner lager was promoted as a healthy substitute for spirits due to its low alcohol percentage by temperance movements in the United States and the Netherlands in the late nineteenth century. For United States, see: Maureen Ogle, *Ambitious Brew: The Story of American Beer* (New York: Harcourt, Inc., 2006), 33–4. For the Netherlands, see: Richard Unger, *A History of Brewing in Holland, 900-1900: Economy, Technology, and the State* (Leiden; Boston: Brill, 2001), 370.

the same clear beverage every time, unlike when ordering a British beer that would be of higher alcohol, very bitter or hoppy, and likely full of sediment due to the lack of extended aging of the beer and poor filtration. Of these qualities, the low ABV (alcohol-by-volume) percentage was most important because it allowed people to drink more without the heavy inebriating effects that were felt with the stronger British ales. This led to the promotion of pilsner drinking by several temperance organizations in Europe and the United States who felt that the golden lagers were less inebriating, and therefore safer and healthier, than spirits and strong ales.[10]

News of the pilsner-style, as well as the actual product, traveled widely due to broader and faster transportation and communication during this period.[11] The development of global trading systems and the spread of Western European dominance through imperialism and colonization helped to promote the products of industrialized powers, including the pilsner. In fact, the pilsner became the dominant beer even within British colonies.

Similarly, export strategies of Continental breweries were much more systematic than that of British breweries. For example, German brewing literature from the late nineteenth century consistently highlighted where German lager beer had been seen, whether it was in Paris or in Buenos Aires. This is symptomatic of the fact that while the British export trade existed for centuries and continued during the nineteenth century, British brewers expended considerably less energy in promoting and selling their products abroad when compared with the Continental lager brewers.

This is the story of how the pilsner beer became the dominant beer in the world less than fifty years after the creation of the first pilsner in 1842. By continuing to focus on domestic traditions of brewing and by refusing to adapt to changing tastes in export markets, the British brewing industry lost its status as the global front-runner. In contrast, Continental brewers readily adopted the latest science, technology, and business strategies in their production of golden lagers for domestic and foreign consumption.

---

[10] Oogle, *Ambitious Brew*, 30, 34–5; Unger, *A History of Brewing in Holland, 900–1900 Economy, Technology, and the State*, 370.

[11] For more on global markets and technology, see: Michael Adas, *Machines as the Measure of Men: Science, Technology, and Ideologies of Western Dominance* (Ithaca: Cornell University Press, 1989) and Steven Topik and Allen Wells, *Global Markets Transformed, 1870–1945* (Cambridge, MA: The Belknap Press of Harvard University Press, 2014).

Through these adoptions, the popularity of pilsner beer was able to spread far outside Europe, and Continental brewers soon sought control over export markets. This led to foreign markets copying the Continental pilsner-style and producing their own golden lagers for local consumption instead of choosing to produce British-style ales.

I contend that the spread and domination of the pilsner cannot be fully understood without attention to both the industrialization of Continental brewing industries and the decline in British influence as an industrial power in the last third of the nineteenth century, even as British imperial might was at its highest point. At this point, however, we have more information on the actions of British and Continental brewing industries in isolation than on the connections and competitions between them over export markets. Historians including Peter Mathias, T. R. Gourvish and R. G. Wilson have focused on the business tactics and domestic market control of the British brewing industry.[12] Mikuláš Teich has devoted most of his attention to the industrialization of the German brewing industry over the course of the nineteenth century.[13] This project takes a wider, and more inclusive, view of the industrialization of these brewing industries, seeking to understand not just the development and spread of lager beers on the Continent in comparison with ale production in Great Britain, but more importantly, how complex networks of trade embedded in European imperialism affected the control of British colonial beer markets.

The spread of pilsner beer did not happen in isolation on the European Continent but included trade networks and European migration across the world. European revolutions that led to mass migrations away from the Continent, as well as imperialism, played a key role in the spread of golden lagers to many different locations including new destinations in the Americas and the many European colonies in the Southern Hemisphere. Imperial trade networks, fueled by colonial settlement and metropolitan economies, were essential to the foundation of British and German breweries in many of these colonies and the spread of specific styles of beer and production methods.

---

[12] Mathias, *The Brewing Industry in England 1700–1830*; Gourvish and Wilson, *The British Brewing Industry, 1830–1980*.

[13] Teich, *Bier, Wissenschaft und Wirtschaft in Deutschland 1800–1914*.

Central to my argument is that the pilsner, the original light golden lager, represents the first modern, industrial, global beer style. The acceptance and desire for this beer in diverse global markets cannot be understood without comprehending how transnational and transcolonial ideas of progress and modernity influenced perceptions of taste and aided in the promotion of a style regardless of the strength of any singular brand or brewery.

In this case, taste triumphed over nationalism in the British colonies, while German nationalism was consistent with taste in migrant communities around the world. The conceptions underpinning taste for golden lagers were fueled and nourished by the scientific and technological innovations promoted by Continental brewers. And it was the lack of attention by British brewers to the growing colonial beer markets that led me to consider the implications of taste over nationalism within British imperial culture regarding consumptive choices of settlers. For the adoption of pilsner beer to succeed in British settlement colonies, taste had to triumph over colonists' loyalty to their empire's own breweries and beer styles. While many settlers went to great lengths to retain a high level of "Britishness" through the purchase of imperial commodities such as cotton and foodstuffs, they did not do so in their choices of beer.[14] Ties to the metropole included the use of English as the official language, British-style education, and trade relations. Indeed, with regard to business opportunities, the brewing industry of the metropole was an outlier in its lack of colonial market interest and influence considering the needs of colonists to have most of their manufactured goods, as well as brewing ingredients, imported. The break between British settlers and their country of origin in terms of beer consumption is a unique element of the colonial experience.

Until now, histories of beer, brewing, and alcohol have overwhelmingly focused either on national, regional, colonial, or metropolitan contexts, but never on the larger global connections of trade, migration, and empire. By examining the different regional and national approaches to brewing styles, science, and technology and showing the larger connections outside of the national

---

[14] For more on British colonial markets and control over them see Jeremy Prestholdt, *Domesticating the World: African Consumerism and the Genealogies of Globalization* (Berkeley: University of California Press, 2008); Aaron L. Friedberg, *The Weary Titan: Britain and the Experience of Relative Decline, 1895–1905* (Princeton, NJ: Princeton University Press, 1988); Alexander Nützenadel and Frank Trentmann, *Food and Globalization: Consumption, Markets and Politics in the Modern World* (Oxford; New York: Berg, 2008).

boundaries we can understand how this specific commodity became divorced of its origins by consumptive and productive choices, if not by name. By using beer as a lens to support my argument that empire and imperial connections were influenced by global networks of trade and diplomatic relationships we can further understand how a food and/or drink like beer may be utilized to understand human connections beyond strict nationalist identities.

For much of the period between 1884 and 1914, metropolitan influence from European nations on their colonies included direct investment through infrastructure development and formalized institutions of political and cultural control over subject populations. However, the consumptive choices made by both colonized and settler populations were influenced by other nations through trade. These consumptive choices had important effects on colonial and metropolitan economies as well as on identities. This is especially important when rival nations or empires benefited from the control of markets assumed by the colony's metropole to be their own, much like the German brewing industry benefited from the spread of pilsner to the detriment of the British.

Although the rise to dominance of golden lager beers was at its height in the 1890s, this book begins with the British brewing industry in the latter half of the eighteenth century. Until the 1860s, British brewers were the best in the world with their utilization of the latest technology, science, and capital accumulation and investment when compared with brewing in Germany during the same period. The stark contrast between the British and German brewing industries during the first half of the nineteenth century makes the later global dominance of the German brewers and the pilsner-style that much more surprising. The reasons for the ascendance of the pilsner-style can only be understood in reference to the decisions made by the British brewing firms in this earlier period. In Chapter 2, I identify the importance of science and technology in the spread of the pilsner-style from 1870 to the end of the century in Europe. As a result of the push for the acceptance of the latest scientific breakthroughs and the development and use of the latest technologies in brewing, German and other Continental brewing industries were able to produce consistent golden lagers that spread in popularity across the region and abroad. In comparison, the British brewing industry retained a traditional focus on its own methods of brewing without taking into account the use of these same innovative developments so popular in Continental breweries, even though brewers were aware of their existence.

The incorporation of the latest science and technology, however, was costly. In order to build and outfit new lager breweries across Europe, brewers and brewing companies needed educated workers and a lot of investment capital. Chapter 3 shows that it was only through forming Limited Liability Companies (*Atkienbrauerei*) with large amounts of capital investment that lager brewers were able to build breweries that could maximize economies of scale to produce quality lager sold at lower prices for local and foreign consumption. In addition, the formalized education of brewers in Germany was supported through federal and private investment so that brewery employees understood and knew of the latest in brewing science and technology. British breweries, however, were run by family firms and worked by apprentices who learned through hands-on experience without the support of courses in science or new technological equipment.

Chapter 4 examines how failed European revolutions and economic hardship in the 1830s and late 1840s led to the mass migration of Germans to the Americas in search of more stable lives and livelihoods. In the course of German settlement in the United States and Latin America they established numerous breweries that brought the pilsner to new regions of the world, far from its European origin.

Chapter 5 focuses on how the pilsner expanded from Continental breweries to the British colonies in India, South Africa, and Australia. News of the pilsner-style, as well as the actual product, traveled widely due to broader and faster transportation and communication during this period. The development of global trading systems and the spread of Western European dominance through imperialism and colonization helped to promote the products of imperial powers, including the pilsner. One argument for the motivation of imperialism by the British is individual wealth by gentleman capitalists through the exportation of manufactured goods from metropoles in Europe to colonies around the world and the control of foreign markets. However, though arguments promoting gentlemanly capitalism concentrate on British interests Germany was more successful than Great Britain at promoting and selling its products abroad, even in contemporary and former British colonies.

Chapter 6 brings together Europe and South Africa in an analysis of taste. Science, technology, investment, and education point to reasons *how* the pilsner spread so quickly and completely in the second half of the nineteenth century, but this chapter explains *why*. The qualities of the pilsner beer helped the popularity of lagers reach new audiences and consumers of beer. Aesthetically, the golden lager has several key points that drew new consumers and pulled them away from the British ales. Pilsner beer is light in body, has a clear and golden color, high levels of carbonation and, perhaps most importantly, a much lower alcohol percentage compared with nineteenth-century British beer. These physical qualities were not possible to attain without the use of new science and technology and act as telling reminders of how the pilsner was the first truly modern beer. Pilsner represented both progress and modernity through its production process and the methods employed by Continental brewers while British beer represented the past and old-fashioned traditions.

This final chapter examines the consumer preferences that explain *why* people chose the pilsner over all other styles of beer. Scholars in a variety of fields, including history, sociology, and anthropology, have demonstrated that the choices people make in terms of food and drink are quite complex. Choosing what to eat and drink is the result of many factors including the consumer's identity, matters of convenience including price, and concern over the consequences of what consumers take into their bodies. Among the most important factors influencing such choices, however, is taste. This chapter explains the reasons why pilsner became the first global beer style in terms of taste. While earlier chapters examine how the pilsner developed and spread through science, technology, education, and business strategies, this chapter explores the reasons people chose (or did not choose) to purchase and drink this style of beer over all others. I argue that the physical attributes of the pilsner—its color, clarity, alcoholic strength, and level of carbonation—combined with a perceived status as the beer of modernity to elevate this style above the other beer choices, especially British ales.

> "The Pilsner ... the beer is incomparable; there is nothing like it elsewhere in the world."[15]
>
> – Mark Twain for *Cosmopolitan* (1898)

---

[15] Mark Twain, "At the Appetite-Cure," *Cosmopolitan* (New York, Vol. 25 (4), August 1898), 425.

1

Ales for Everyone: English and Continental Brewing Industries, 1750–1870

Introduction

Before the global reign of the golden lager by Continental brewing industries, the British brewing industry was the best in the world in both quality and quantity. From the late eighteenth century and through the middle of the nineteenth century the British brewing industry led beer production in the world using technological innovation, innovative production methods, and the adoption of new business strategies. Up through the 1860s it was the British brewing industry that was at the forefront of producing consistent, high-quality beer. In a world where beer consistency was difficult, even impossible in many cases, producing a reliable product is what made the British brewers the best.

In fact, without the inventions and innovations brought about by the industrialization of the British brewers, Continental brewers would not have gained the knowledge, experience, or technology to produce the golden lagers that came to dominate the world by the turn of the twentieth century. Without understanding the nature of the European brewing industries up to the 1870s, the reason for the spread of the pilsner-style does not make sense. The pilsner did not suddenly appear in the city of Pilsen in 1842 and spread of its own accord: rather, its creation was only possible through the earlier work of British brewers and the adoption and further innovation by Continental brewers through the early and mid-nineteenth century. As this chapter shows, the British brewing industry was the most innovative in terms of production methods by utilizing new technology and new business tactics that incorporated inventive investment strategies. These methods and strategies propelled British brewers to the highest level of quality beer production in the world and influenced the Continental brewing industries, who would eventually eclipse the British by the end of the nineteenth century.

Without the innovations developed through the industrial production of the porter style in the UK, the pilsner—which came to be known for its quality and consistency—would not have been possible. In several ways, the stories of the porter and pilsner are comparable. Both styles arose and gained in popularity at a time of national industrialization—Britain for the porter and Germany for pilsner. Both became popular across class lines, and both gained regional prominence above all other available styles due to newly possible economies of scale that made for a cheaper and better-quality product than most other options. However, while the porter's popularity waned rather quickly in the early nineteenth century, the golden lagers continue to hold sway worldwide into the twenty-first century. While porter was one of the first industrial beer styles, pilsner is the first truly modern beer style due to pilsner brewers' use of the latest scientific knowledge and technology developed and adopted through the spreading industrialization of the late nineteenth century. The pilsner-style's continued legacy as *the* global style is a traceable marker of globalization, which was certainly not a foregone conclusion at the beginning of the nineteenth century considering the limited technological state of brewing industries on the Continent at the time.

This chapter begins with a brief overview of what beer is and how it is produced, in order for the reader to understand the differences between ale and lager and their differing systems of production in the nineteenth century. It then moves to a history of the British brewing industry as it developed up to the 1870s through an examination of its technologies, business structures, and export trade. The following section deals with an examination of the German/Continental brewing industry and explains who the major brewers were and how they acquired the knowledge necessary for the production of the first pilsner in 1842 in Pilsen, Bohemia, within the Austrian Empire. By looking at the British and Central European brewing industries side-by-side, we can see the strengths of the British brewing industry at this time as well as the establishment of necessary prerequisites for the spread of golden lagers later in the nineteenth century.

How to Brew Beer: A Basic Description

The basic steps of beer production and brewing have remained relatively constant over time. However, the industrialization of brewing beginning in the mid-eighteenth century and the introduction of scientific knowledge and new technologies have made the brewing process more efficient and less labor-intensive while producing a more consistent and higher quality product. What follows is a simplified description of the beer brewing process at the turn of the nineteenth century in Great Britain.

While there are many ingredients that go into the creation of standard beer, a basic recipe includes the four simple ingredients that make up the *Reinheitsgebot*, or German Beer Purity Law: water, malted grain, hops, and yeast. When combined in a specific way and over a certain amount of time, the result is beer. The brewing process begins with the malting of grain, usually barley.[1] This started with barley steeped in warm water to begin germination.[2] Lighter grains floated to the top and were skimmed off for animal feed. After about three days, the water would be drained off and the grain was left for a half day to dry out. The grain would then be placed in square wooden receptacles known as the "couch" and left for 20–30 hours, during which time excise officers would measure the volume of grain for taxing purposes. After this, the grain would be evenly spread, at a depth less than one foot, across the malting floor and allowed to germinate. Maltsters would regularly turn the grain with wide shovels for twelve to fifteen days to make sure the grain received the right amount of air, heat, and light to encourage germination and avoid the growth of mold. Oftentimes the grain was sprinkled with water to maintain the right level of moisture.[3]

The malting of the grain was complete when germination was arrested, and the grains were dried upon a kiln over heat. Higher temperatures would dry

---

[1] Barley became the main grain for beer production both because it proved to be a good grain for malting and for providing the right kind of sugars for fermentation into alcohol and because it was seen as a lesser grade grain for bread and as food for humans compared with wheat and rye. This was because barley was seen as an animal feed. Mikuláš Teich, *Bier, Wissenschaft und Wirtschaft in Deutschland 1800–1914: ein Beitrag zur deutschen Industrialisierungsgeschichte* (Wien: Böhlau, 2000), 16.

[2] Today the accepted temperature for this process is between 14 and 20° Celsius, or 57–68° Fahrenheit.

[3] Peter Mathias, *The Brewing Industry in England, 1700–1830* (England: Cambridge University Press, 1959), 407.

the grains more quickly, but usually led to darker malt that produced darker beer with burnt or roasted flavors. The use of a high percentage of dark malt would also produce beer of lower alcohol than a beer that used lighter-colored pale malt because lighter malts had more fermentable sugar available.[4] Before the industrial efficiency of coal and steam power in the breweries the grains would be dried over a fire. Fires, however, were difficult to control and resulted in the grains averaging out to a dull brown color. However, by using coal (and later, coke) and steam, the maltsters had better control over the temperature levels and the malt would not lose as much sugar as over a hot and uneven fire. Similarly, the later development of indirect heated kilns aided in this and allowed other sources of heat to be used so that any smoke would never be in contact with the malt and affect later flavors in the beer.[5]

In the brewhouse, the next stage was mashing. British brewers, who used the infusion method, took the malted grain, and let it steep in hot water in order to extract the fermentable sugar (maltose being the most abundant) from the grains. Mashing was usually done multiple times to extract as much sugar as possible. Each "run" of liquid was used for a different beer. The first extraction was the strongest because the most fermentable sugar was available. This produced the strongest, highest alcohol beer. The second mash would either be added to the first run or be used for a middle-strength beer. The third and final mash would be used to create a "small" or "mild" beer that would be very low in alcohol.[6]

Once mashing was complete, the liquid, known as the liquor, was brought to a boil in a boiling kettle and hops were added. Usually, the boil continued for at least sixty minutes or up to a few hours. Hops were added several times throughout the boil depending on how bitter, or "hoppy," the brewers intended the beer to taste. Normally, hops were added three times at the beginning of the boil, in the middle or around twenty minutes before the end, and at the end or immediately after the boil was stopped. The liquid was now called "wort" and was rapidly cooled to 68–72°F (20–22°C). In early nineteenth-century Britain,

---

[4] Mathias, *The Brewing Industry in England, 1700–1830*, 411; this is similar to how lightly roasted coffee beans have more caffeine.

[5] Leandro Meiners, "Empire in a Bottle," email, April 13, 2020.

[6] T. R. Gourvish and R. G. Wilson, *The British Brewing Industry, 1830–1980* (Cambridge [England]; New York: Cambridge University Press, 1994), 42.

this was done by pumping the wort to the top of the brewery to big, open containers for cooling. This process was much more difficult in summer before mechanized refrigeration. Steam often condensed on dusty beams above the cooling containers, which could lead to acidic and irregular fermentation if the dust fell into the cooling wort. Once cooled, brewers added yeast to the wort, and fermentation was allowed to begin.[7]

Fermentation can take anywhere from a few days to a few weeks depending upon the style of beer being made. Yeast is a single-celled living organism that ingests available fermentable sugars and excretes carbon dioxide and ethanol. Depending on how much fermentable material was in the wort, the resulting beer could contain various strengths of alcohol. Once the brewer decided that the fermentation was complete using a hydrometer to measure lower, and stable, specific gravity caused by the conversion of fermentable sugars to ethanol, the beer was transferred, or "racked," to another vessel to age and clarify. This process could take days, weeks, or months depending upon the style of beer being produced. Many brewers used metal vessels, but some also used wooden barrels also known as casks. When the beer was ready, it was either bottled or put into casks for distribution.

Ale vs. Lager

Though the process of beer brewing is very similar regardless of style, there is a necessary distinction that must be made between ales and lagers. The differences are what came to separate nearly all of the brewing industries of Britain and the Continent, which makes the popularity and spread of the golden lager that much more extraordinary considering the greater difficulty in its production when compared with British ales.

Though there are many *styles* of beer, nearly all can be divided into two categories based upon the kind of yeast that is used during fermentation. These are ales and lagers. The beers produced by the majority of the British brewing industry were ales, while the Continental beers, including the pilsner, were lager beers. These distinctions had important ramifications for the brewing

---

[7] Gourvish and Wilson, *The British Brewing Industry, 1830–1980*, 54.

processes in these two regions and for any brewery that decided to produce lagers in any other part of the world, especially for ones with warm climates.

Ales have been the most prominent category of beer throughout much of human history because warmer temperatures allow for easier fermentation for the wild yeasts found in nature, which made ales easier to make and required less temperature control to produce a decent product. Ale yeasts rise to the surface of fermenting wort and ferment at higher temperatures than lager yeasts, between 59 and 72°F (15–22°C). Fermentation would take only three to seven days to be complete and then the beer could either be aged or sold right away depending on the style. Due to the top fermentation, the wort needed to be covered and watched carefully so that any airborne yeasts and bacteria would not spoil the beer. The British breweries focused on producing styles of ale including brown ales, porters, stouts, pale ales, and India Pale Ales, many of which were developed, or named after-the-fact, between 1750 and 1830 and continued to be the primary styles throughout the nineteenth century. However, in Bavaria the top-fermenting brewing systems were only in universal use until about the 1840s.[8]

In contrast, lager yeasts ferment at the bottom of the fermentation vessels, which makes it easier to avoid contamination by airborne bacteria and wild yeasts during fermentation. Lager yeast was hybridized during the early modern era in Bavaria due to laws against brewing beer in warm weather to prevent what came to be understood as bacterial contamination.[9] Brewers stored the beer in caves filled with ice where fermentation occurred slowly over the winter. The lager yeast fermented at the lower temperatures, between 43 and 54°F (6–12°C), which required some level of temperature control whether through brewing only during the coldest months of the year, utilizing ice caves, or after the 1870s operating mechanized refrigeration apparatuses. Due to the lower temperature, the lager yeasts also fermented at a slower speed, taking up to three weeks for a single batch of beer. Once fermentation was

---

[8] Mikulas Teich, "The Industrialization of Brewing in Germany (1800–1914)," in *Production, Marketing, and Consumption of Alcoholic Beverages since the Late Middle Ages: Session B-14: Proceedings, Tenth International Economic History Congress, Leuven, August 1990*, eds., Aerts Erik Cullen L. M. Wilson R. G. International Economic History Congress, (Leuven University Press, 1990), 130–40.

[9] Jeffrey Pilcher, "'Tastes like Horse Piss': Asian Encounters with European Beer," in *Gastronomica: The Journal of Critical Food Studies*, Vol. 16 (1), 29.

complete, the beer would then have to be *lagered* (lager being German for "to store") for many months until it reached the desired level of clarity, carbonation, and flavor for consumption. Considering the greater needs of lager brewing both in equipment and quality temperature control in comparison to ales, the spread of lagers does not seem obvious at first, let alone a foregone conclusion. However, the choices and strategies taken by investors and brewers of lagers in Continental Europe, and then abroad, explain how and why this was possible.

One more distinction must be made in terms of British ales. Brewing at the beginning of the eighteenth century included a number of different types of malt liquor. The terms beer and ale were used then, as they are today, as generic words for malt liquor. However, each term implied a different commodity to brewers and merchants of the eighteenth and nineteenth century. After the development of the London Porter and stout in the mid-eighteenth century, beer came to represent this "new city drink … which was thick, black, and stored for several months." In contrast, the word ale was attached to "clearer, lighter coloured 'ales' of the provinces which were drunk much 'younger' than porter."[10]

Part I: Industrialization of Brewing in Great Britain

The industrialization of the British brewing industry eventually helped in the industrialization of the Continental brewing industries. Without the innovations in beer production in Britain the development of the pilsner would likely have taken much longer. This section deals with the earlier British industrialization and the innovations in technology utilized by porter beer brewers in London that were able to be effectively used by Continental brewers in the nineteenth century as they developed lager brewing.

The industrialization of beer brewing in the UK began in the eighteenth century and led to fundamental changes in its structure. With the rise in production and consumption of the porter style there was also a complete shift in the center of economic activity from small-scale, independent brewers to large brewing firms based primarily in London and then Burton-Upon-Trent.

---

[10] Mathias, *The Brewing Industry in England, 1700–1830*, 5.

Porter brewing led to changes in the scale of production while also providing new opportunities for brewers and entrepreneurs. Two important features of porter made these changes possible: first, the greater stability of the product and, second, higher levels of urbanization and industrial organization in towns around England.[11]

Though there were several styles of beer being produced in the UK during this time, only porter brewers rose to high levels of production in the eighteenth century and led to the establishment of a modern brewing industry. One of the principal reasons for this is that porter was the first beer technically suited for mass-production at then-contemporary standards of control.[12]

British beer drinkers had a preference for beer higher in alcohol that was the product of traditional tastes, which developed over centuries through combinations of local malts, water, yeasts, and brewing production methods. The strong English beers were a reaction to consumer demands that involved heavy and irregular drinking bouts during the pre-industrial calendar.[13] Beers that were stronger in alcohol helped consumers feel warmer in colder weather before the arrival of railroads and regular coal deliveries. In addition, the strength of the beer made up for the overall low quality of the product.[14]

The benefit of large-scale porter brewing was that it was not delicate in color or taste, which made it more manageable in brewing with primitive industrial machinery and easier to hide the use of cheaper ingredients. The brewing materials—grains, hops, etc.—were also utilized more rigorously than lighter ale brewing and included less fine barley and lower grade hops. Porter was thicker, blacker, more bitter, and stronger than any similarly priced beer.[15] This metropolitan specialty used malted grains roasted at high temperature, which made the beer dark and cloudy. The porter would be aged in large vats for nine or more months before sale because consumers enjoyed the flavor of aged, "stale" beer.[16]

---

[11] Mathias, *The Brewing Industry in England, 1700–1830*, 11.
[12] Mathias, *The Brewing Industry in England, 1700–1830*, 13.
[13] E. P. Thompson, "Time, Work-Discipline, and Industrial Capitalism," in *Past & Present*, No. 38, 1967, 76.
[14] Gourvish and Wilson, *The British Brewing Industry, 1830–1980*, 42.
[15] Mathias, *The Brewing Industry in England, 1700–1830*, 413.
[16] Gourvish and Wilson, *The British Brewing Industry, 1830–1980*, 79.

As production facilities became larger over the course of the English Industrial Revolution, the brewing vessels also grew in size. With a greater volume of wort, the porter could withstand a greater quantity of heat as well, which allowed porter brewers in London to extend their brewing season from early September to mid-June in comparison with the early October to mid-May season of the Burton-Upon-Trent brewers further north. In addition, higher levels of hops and grain also helped the porter tolerate more heat without deterioration compared to ale. Another technical advantage for the porter was that once fermentation had begun the brewers allowed the yeast enough time to ferment all of the available sugars, which left the finished beer drier to the taste and with less possibility of attracting wild yeasts that could spoil the beer. In comparison, ale brewers would arrest the fermentation before all of the fermentable sugars had been consumed. This left the ale tasting sweeter but made it less stable as it aged.[17] Yet, one of the most important aspects of porter was its stability in comparison with ales, a factor that may have played a determining role in the rise of mass-production in the brewing industry. The robustness of porter both in the brewing and fermentation processes and in its shelf life helped it to be the beer of choice for British consumers through the beginning of the nineteenth century.[18]

This robustness proved important as the scale of production increased. More wort meant more heat and a much slower process when lowering the temperature from the boiling. Without any devices to regulate the temperature within fermentation vessels, the increased temperature could have very detrimental effects on the fermentation itself. This was similar to difficulties with brewing beer in the summer when the higher temperatures could lead to both poor fermentation but also off-flavors of the final product. Porter beer was able to tolerate a greater amount of heat than ale without deterioration, even allowing porter brewers to continue production into warmer months of the year compared with ale brewers. However, in the beginning of the nineteenth century, once brewers were able to take better control of fermentation with ales using new equipment like thermometers, saccharometers, and attemperation coils, the technical advantage of porter was mostly removed.[19]

---

[17] Mathias, *The Brewing Industry in England, 1700–1830*, 17–18.
[18] Mathias, *The Brewing Industry in England, 1700–1830*, 18–19.
[19] Mathias, *The Brewing Industry in England, 1700–1830*, 19.

In addition to the role of porter in supporting the growth of brewing facilities and the size of production and consumption of a specific style of beer, the later eighteenth century also witnessed important changes in the structure of the brewing industry in London. While there were modest changes in the total quantities and the number of brewers in London, there were great changes in the distribution of the amounts of beer brewed in individual breweries. Due to new efficiencies of large-scale production, the relative change in relation to modest aggregate expansion of production distinguished the revolution of the brewing industry from other industries like cotton and iron.[20] What this means is that while the beginning of the eighteenth century saw many smaller brewers producing modest amounts of beer and ale for local consumers, by the end of the century there were only a few brewers producing very large amounts of beer. Between 1800 and 1830, only five brewers produced three-quarters of all the porter, compared to the twelve largest brewers together producing 383,000 out of 915,000 barrels of strong beer and ale in 1748.[21]

Between 1750 and 1830, brewing was technically more suited than many other manufacturing processes for the development of mass-production methods due to the methods of handling and the forms of power available at the time. Two central aspects promoted the expansion of this industry. The first was a strong local market in London that supported large production through mass distribution and mass consumption. The second was the porter style itself, being a stable product that was able to withstand expansion of production and distribution. These key elements led to a greater profit for porter brewers through their changing methods of brewing and expanding brewing capacities. The success brought about through the brewing of porter allowed the brewing entrepreneurs to reach levels of size and ambition that had never before been seen in Great Britain, or even the world.[22]

---

[20] Mathias, *The Brewing Industry in England, 1700–1830*, 22.

[21] These brewers were Whitbread, Thrale, Truman, Sir William and Felix Calvert, and Hammond. Mathias, *The Brewing Industry in England, 1700–1830*, 23, 25–6.

[22] Mathias, *The Brewing Industry in England, 1700–1830*, 37–8.

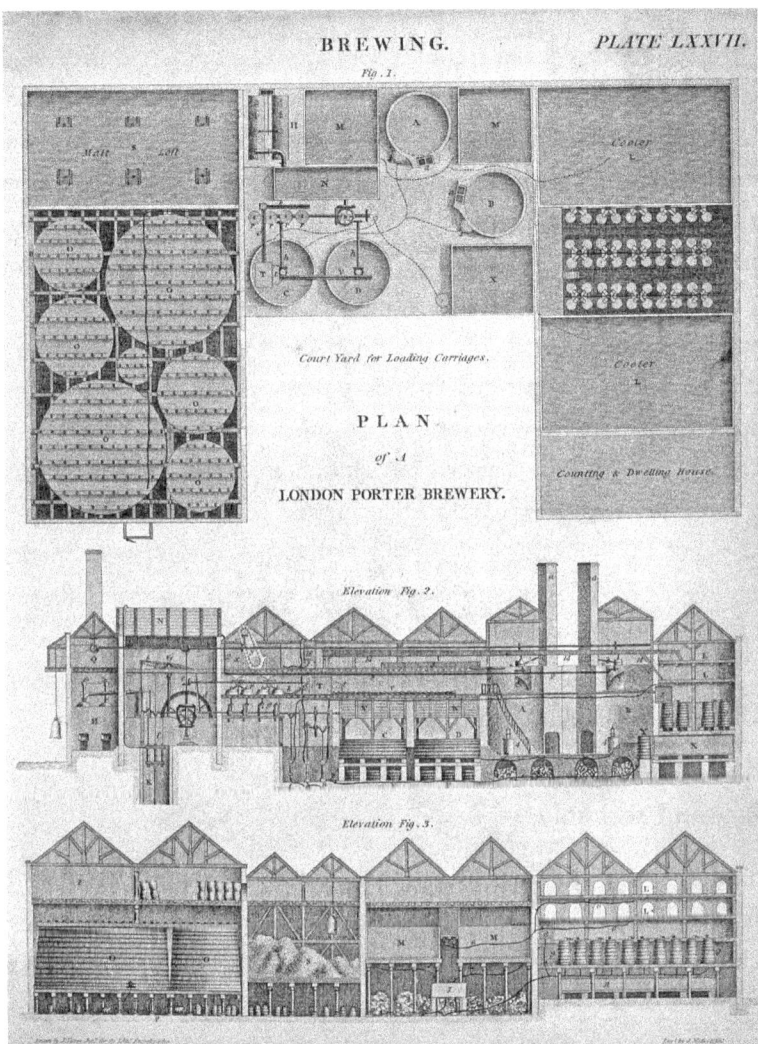

Figure 1.1 London Porter Brewery.

One of the new efficiencies that occurred in brewing at this time was the design and positioning of vessels within the brewhouse. Though most breweries today are designed horizontally with the different brewing vessels next to each other at the same level of brewery, it was more efficient to build a brewery in a vertical design before the advent of efficient pumping systems that we have today. As mentioned above, once the mashing was complete, the grain removed, and the boiling complete, the finished wort would be moved to the top of the brewery so that it could cool as quickly as possible. The rest of the brewing process would then use gravity to move the beer from fermentation to the eventual packaging in bottles or wooden barrels. Through the efficiency of design, brewers were able to increase the size and scale of their brewing from the 1760s onward. An important effect of this was that accuracy became visible with better control of temperature and specific gravities of the wort.[23] In addition, through design efficiency in the handling of the product, labor expenses and time were cut down while increasing the rate of production with the added benefit of better-quality beer. Porter was the only beer able to be produced under these new conditions and only a small group of brewers were able to do it successfully. The critical minimum barrelage to produce at the most economical scale rose quickly during the latter half of the eighteenth century and the initial capital needed to break into the porter market at efficient levels of production became much greater.[24] This meant that fewer brewers were making much larger quantities of beer and were able to keep out most new porter competition, a trend Continental lager brewers would copy later in the nineteenth century.[25]

Science and Technology

With new technology, British brewers were able to surpass the brewing efforts of all other nations. The new technologies developed during the Industrial Revolution from the mid-eighteenth through the mid-nineteenth century put British ales at a level of precision and consistency that no other brewing nation could match. New inventions brought to the brewing process helped the brewers produce beers that could be reliably regular in their flavor profiles

---

[23] Specific Gravity refers to the change in density between the wort and finished beer that tallies the amount of fermentable sugars converted into ethanol. Control over the gravity allows the brewer to make sure of the strength of the finished product leading to a more consistent beer.

[24] Mathias, *The Brewing Industry in England, 1700–1830*, 42–3.

[25] The one porter brewery they couldn't keep out was the Guinness Brewing Co. out of Dublin, Ireland. For more on this see Andy Bielenberg, "Irish Brewing Industry and the Rise of Guinness, 1790–1914," in *The Dynamics of the International Brewing Industry since 1800*, eds. R. G. Wilson and T. R. Gourvish (New York: Routledge, 1998). Chapter 7.

and alcoholic strength. Beer consumers and producers around the world recognized the British for being at the forefront of modern brewing. This was due to the invention and acceptance of thermometers, saccharometers, and attemperation by British brewers that made consistency of product possible. In a world where beer consistency was difficult, even impossible in many cases, producing a reliable product is what made the British brewers the best at this time.

With increased scale, the first generation of industrialists exploited their commercial success of porters to organize their breweries in such a way to capitalize on large-scale production and distribution. However, there were certain problems with increasing the scale, especially in terms of accurate measurement of materials including grain, water, hops, etc. Considering that beer had never before been brewed in such quantities for such a large population of consumers, it was essential that the brewers keep their position in the markets through the production of a product of consistent high-quality through accurate measurements and systematic processing because it would also mean a much bigger loss if a batch went bad.[26]

British brewers between 1750 and 1850 were at the forefront of brewing technology with their implementation of scientific instruments to industrial brewing including the thermometer and saccharometer. Thermometers came into general use by the 1780s. Before their use brewers used a steam test to determine when the mash had reached the correct temperature. This meant that the brewer would boil the water and once the steam settled to a point that the brewer could see his face in the liquid, they would add the grain. However, even with the wider acceptance of thermometers in the UK brewers could not agree on the best temperature for mashing, even seventy years later. In the 1830s, English brewers usually kept the mashing temperature at 168°–170°F (75.6–76.7°C) while in 1840, Scottish brewers would still keep their grains in water for four hours at 178°–190°F (81–87.8°C).[27]

Even with these disparities, the thermometer was the first to be adopted because it allowed a new regularity to the process of brewing that did not

---

[26] Mathias, *The Brewing Industry in England, 1700–1830*, 63–4.
[27] We know now that the fermentable sugar, diastase, begins to be destroyed above 170°F. Gourvish and Wilson, *The British Brewing Industry, 1830–1980*, 51.

change or violate any traditional process.[28] The saccharometer, however, caused a bigger stir. Saccharometers measure the concentration of sugar in a solution, which in the brewing process meant that the specific gravity (S.G.), or density and strength of the wort and beer could be accurately measured, both by brewers and by the excise authorities who made sure the brewers paid the correct amount of taxes on their malt and beer. In spite of significant distrust in innovations, most brewers in England had adopted saccharometers by 1805.[29] However, in Ireland in 1812 no one had even heard of them, let alone begun including them as part of the brewing process.[30] Technical writings, including John Richardson's *Statistical estimates of the materials of brewing etc.*, first produced in 1784, helped spread the use and understanding of saccharometers as a means for determining consistent strength of beer. He argued that brewers had long neglected the progressive decrease of the S.G. in beer during fermentation and called this decrease "attenuation," meaning dilution. Decades before Pasteur published *Études sur la bière*, Richardson was arguing that through use of saccharometers brewers could understand the transformation of fermentables in the transition from wort to beer and thus understand fermentation itself. He then explained that the strength of each beer is proportionate to the dilution of wort—or decrease of the S.G.—during fermentation.[31]

With the inclusion of temperature control and the ability to know how much fermentable material was in the wort and finished beer English brewing reached a level of industrial progress that no other national brewing industry could match or replicate. The saccharometer made possible several important innovations in the brewing process for the English. It allowed the meticulous pricing on cost quality through knowing the amount of fermentable matter in parcels of malt and worts, which could be adjusted to maintain a regularity of strength in the beer. In addition, excise commissioners could exact

---

[28] Mathias, *The Brewing Industry in England, 1700–1830*, 67.
[29] Teich, *Bier, Wissenschaft und Wirtschaft in Deutschland 1800–1914*, 59.
[30] Mathias, *The Brewing Industry in England, 1700–1830*, 72.
[31] John Richardson, *Statistical Estimates of the Materials of Brewing, or, a Treatise on the Application and Use of the Saccharometer: An Instrument Constructed for the Purposes of Regulating to Advantage the Oeconomy of the Brewhouse, and of Establishing the Means of Producing Uniform Strength in Malt-liquors* (London: Printed for G. Robinson ..., J. Sewell ..., T. Browne, at Hull, C. Elliott, at Edinburgh, Luke White, at Dublin, and T. White, at Cork, 1784), 27–8, 151–4.

manipulation of the cost of duty according to the specific gravity of the wort, the standards of which would not be introduced until 1880 by Prime Minister Gladstone.[32]

The next development with thermometers and saccharometers involved a scientific commission of professors from the University of Edinburgh, who were invited by the Scottish Financial Authority to establish values for barley malts and average duties for taxation. The commission included Thomas Thomson, a chemistry professor whose saccharometer design was widely accepted by British brewers. The professors developed a differentiated tax rate based upon barley quality and presented their work in 1806 to the British Parliament. This event solidified the use of saccharometers in the British brewing industry, and the eventual German translation in 1822 of the commission's presentation would have a big impact in the adoption of scientific methods by the German brewing industry.[33]

With the knowledge that thermometers were able to give to brewers, it was not long before other temperature-related innovations were developed by British brewers including the ability to control fermentation through temperature control with attemperators. This began with a proposal from John Long to the Commissioners of Victualing at the naval breweries in February 1791 suggesting a more efficient method of brewing. Long's innovation of temperature control included using lengths of copper tubing to run water at a set temperature within the mash-tun and fermentation vessels made it possible to brew higher quality and more consistent beer in the summer months. In addition, he argued for covering the mash-tun to limit evaporation, a simple suggestion but one that had not been done before. By 1805, most breweries in England had adopted both attemperators and mash-tun coverage.[34] The use of piping was also utilized to cool the wort quickly by passing the hot wort through pipes surrounded by circulating cold water using a patented "refrigerator" developed in 1801 by a brewer named Henry Tickell. Tickell's refrigerators were adopted by many major breweries by 1823.[35]

---

[32] Mathias, *The Brewing Industry in England, 1700–1830*, 73.
[33] Teich, *Bier, Wissenschaft und Wirtschaft in Deutschland 1800–1914*, 61–2.
[34] Mathias, *The Brewing Industry in England, 1700–1830*, 74–5.
[35] Mathias, *The Brewing Industry in England, 1700–1830*, 75.

Figure 1.2 A Brewhouse Yard.

Initially, heat-exchange systems were very expensive so many British brewers continued to use cooling squares like those discussed earlier that would sit at the top of the brewery. The purpose for rapid cooling of the wort was to avoid oxidation and contamination. Quickly cooling the wort inhibits these problems that lead to off-flavors and quicker spoilage in the finished beer. Brewing during the summer months using attemperators and refrigerators was finally accepted and used by the larger brewers by the 1830s.[36]

The adoption of these new technologies into the brewing process occurred during a change in the public taste for porter beginning in 1790. Through the mid to late-eighteenth century, porters produced in London would go through about nine months of storage in large vats before being sent to publicans for

---

[36] Gourvish and Wilson, *The British Brewing Industry, 1830–1980*, 55.

sale to consumers. This timing would be even longer in country trade outside the metropolitan center, or for export because those beers would be stronger and require more time to mellow in flavor for consumers. However, with the introduction of the new technologies and processes the brewers were able to cut this time down to a four- to six-week process by mixing younger beer with the vatted "stale" porter to mimic the old beer taste while retaining a longer shelf life due to their higher alcohol percentage from using pale malted grain.[37]

New technology was not limited to new efficiencies in the brewing process but also to labor-saving mechanizations. While large dray-horses were still needed to transport beer to pubs the use of horses within the breweries declined as the use of steam power became more efficient. For instance, mill horses for grinding down malted grain were no longer necessary with the introduction of steam-powered mills. The first two steam engines installed in London breweries in 1784 paved the way for nearly all of the operations of brewing to become mechanized by 1800.[38] By 1830, nearly all commercial breweries had turned to power mashing, which was more efficient and effective in producing good wort for beer. While the old methods of mashing required two to five successive mashes of the same grain, the new power mashing techniques made it possible to only do one mash with the help of mechanical mashing rakes powered by steam. While the rakes were put into use by the 1790s, sparging machines that effectively mixed the malt and wort thoroughly became popular in the 1830s, first in Scotland and then in England. By the 1860s, mashing had become completely mechanized across the UK.[39]

These new technologies changed many aspects of the brewing process in Britain, though not the overall sequence of production. For instance, porter beers began with the use of cheaper brown malts that would create the dark

---

[37] Mathias, *The Brewing Industry in England, 1700–1830*, 76–7.
[38] Mathias, *The Brewing Industry in England, 1700–1830*, 82.
[39] Gourvish and Wilson, *The British Brewing Industry, 1830–1980*, 51–2.

color and roasted flavor desired by customers. This worked well prior to the use of steam heat and tools of measurement like the saccharometer and thermometer. As breweries became more mechanized and the brewing procedures became more effective, porter brewers began using paler malts of better quality. More skilled malting techniques and better barley allowed the porter brewers to use pale malts that would add more fermentable sugars with less actual grain, which would save the brewers money both in grain purchases as well as taxation that was based upon the amount of malt used. Instead of using only a single grade of cheap dark brown malt, the brewers used smaller amounts of brown malts that had been highly scorched mixed in with the pale malts to bring the desired color and taste of standard porters.[40]

The industrialization of British brewing not only included the use of new scientific apparatuses in the breweries but also the support of trained scientists. After decades of consumer fears over the adulteration of beer, breweries began to employ chemists by 1845 to test their beer and to theorize new techniques for the brewing process. The scientists would work with head brewers to examine and work on barley, starches, and different fermentable sugars in order to produce superior products. Brewers, many of them chemists themselves including Cornelius O'Sullivan at Bass and Peter Griess at Allsopp in Burton-upon-Trent, were at the forefront of this incorporation of scientific knowledge.[41] However, a big difference of what was to come on the Continent was the sharing of knowledge and the development of brewing institutions to share scientific breakthroughs and any of the incremental steps toward better, more consistent, beers. Most of these breweries worked in isolation, especially at this time in the first half of the nineteenth century and saw their work as proprietary and secret for their brewery's benefits only. This was a very different take than what would happen on the Continent, which would have far-reaching consequences for the British brewing industry and its choice of products.

---

[40] Burnt sugars or drugs would also be used to mimic the original porter flavors. Mathias, *The Brewing Industry in England, 1700–1830*, 415–20.

[41] C. C. Owen, *The Greatest Brewery in the World: A History of Bass, Ratcliff & Gretton* (Chesterfield: Derbyshire Record Society, 1992), 86.

Business

Beer production was not only important to the producers and consumers of beer but also to the financial stability of the government. In the early nineteenth century, 18 percent of Britain's total national revenue came from malt and beer taxes. By 1879–80, this grew to 43.5 percent. Brewers developed many strategies between 1750 and 1870 to maintain and grow market shares locally and nationally. However, because British brewers concentrated on their regional markets, they gave little attention to export markets. This choice would have negative effects for the British brewing industry once other nations' brewers began industrializing, and in fact led its decline in nearly every foreign and colonial market by the early 1890s.

One of the most important developments in the late eighteenth century that had deleterious effects for the British brewing industry a hundred years later was the growth of the tied house trade. The tied trade, as it became known, was when a brewery purchased or controlled pubs wherein only its beers were sold. Through either outright ownership or via loans to the publicans the breweries would then have a guaranteed location in which to sell their beers. From the beginning, this investment was not for the purpose of profits in real estate but only to further the interests of brewers in gaining market percentage in (mostly) urban areas.[42] In the late eighteenth and early nineteenth centuries there was a race for tied houses in London between three major breweries: Barclay Perkins, Truman, and Whitbread. Between 1790 and 1830, the amount of money invested in tied houses went from less than £27,000 to over £300,000.[43]

The rush toward tied houses developed out of a need for control over distribution due to some of the peculiar qualities of porter. Considering the need for a year of storage for the porter prior to being sold, the brewers had to be sure they had a stable consumer base once the beer was ready. Also, because of the amount of space needed for production and storage—storage being necessary to reach the right level of "quality"—porter brewing had to be done on a scale large enough for the brewers to derive the full technical advantages from its production, separate from the economic benefits.[44] The growth

---

[42] Mathias, *The Brewing Industry in England, 1700–1830*, 120.
[43] Mathias, *The Brewing Industry in England, 1700–1830*, 300.
[44] Mathias, *The Brewing Industry in England, 1700–1830*, 103.

of the tied houses intensified the home market for British brewers. Porter consumption concentrated in this market, and it was here that industrial and commercial reorganization occurred.

Funding for breweries and brewery expansion was difficult through the early nineteenth century. In order for any joint-stock flotation or incorporation to occur, brewers needed either a private act of Parliament or Letters Patent from the Crown, neither of which were likely to happen due to a lack of influence within the government and monarchy. Brewers often opted for partnerships with bankers or financiers in order to compete through increasing production and buying into the tied trade.[45] While most brewing firms began as family enterprises or smaller partnerships in the middle of the eighteenth century, by the early nineteenth century these firms were led by partnerships of businessmen who generated capital through family and personal business connections, unlike investment through incorporation as the Continental brewers would take advantage of later in the century, and to a lesser extent, the British brewery firms would too at that point. Partnerships that relied on investment through personal and familial connections had several problems that incorporation and professional management would later avoid. For instance, partner successions could be difficult with leadership amounting to something of a lottery depending on who inherited the role of partner. A capacity for business was not an inheritable trait and ensuring continuity of the brewery's direction across generations was not easy.[46] Reputations were paramount to profit strategies as seen by the comment made by an owner of the Truman Brewery that it was "better to acquire now by good beer, than to have to seek it then by gifts, and loans and purchases of leases" for tied houses.[47]

The importance of reputations in the British brewing industry made brewers obsessed with secrecy. Unlike later collaborations that occurred on the Continent, as I examine in detail later, the British used many techniques to prevent possible corporate espionage in their breweries. Many breweries used coded thermometer scales, faked portions of entries in their brewing

---

[45] Mathias, *The Brewing Industry in England, 1700–1830*, 245.
[46] Gourvish and Wilson, *The British Brewing Industry, 1830–1980*, 234.
[47] Gourvish and Wilson, *The British Brewing Industry, 1830–1980*, 229.

books, and made sure to only let the partners of the brewing firm actually see the true accounts. One of the key results of this level of secrecy, however, was that it made innovation difficult.[48] Without collaboration, brewers were unable to learn from each other's mistakes or successes that could enhance their products and efficiencies. In comparison to the home trade, the export trade was relatively unimportant to them, which later led to the domination of the global beer markets by other nations with export-minded brewing firms including Germany and the United States by the end of the nineteenth century. The British brewers focused on tightening their grips on local markets, seeing them as assured profits while foreign markets were less secure. The uncertainty of export markets revolved around the needs of investing in future profits from beer that had to travel extensive distances and may spoil or never arrive.

Export Trade

Beer was one of the accepted parts of life in England. Because of this, travelers and colonists brought it with them to "whatever parts of the globe the call of profit and empire had drawn them."[49] Due to its great bulk and low value, beer was only carried under conditions of water-travel because it was cheaper than travel by land before railroads became more affordable. Open-sea travel presented specific difficulties. Export beer, they thought, needed to be higher in alcohol for their British ales than beer for local markets in order to survive the constant motion of ship travel. Agitation was nearly as bad as heat as a threat to beer quality. While beer exports from England increased between 1750 and 1830, their economic significance declined sharply as the costs to export made it unappealing to most British brewers.[50]

There were three reasons for the decline of beer exports at the beginning of the nineteenth century including international events, the beer preferences of foreign consumers, and the keeping quality of the beer itself. The first was the Napoleonic Wars and the blockade that closed the Baltic Sea trade to brewers in London and England's other major hub, Burton-upon-Trent.

---

[48] Gourvish and Wilson, *The British Brewing Industry, 1830–1980*, 235.
[49] Mathias, *The Brewing Industry in England, 1700–1830*, 139.
[50] Mathias, *The Brewing Industry in England, 1700–1830*, 139.

The Burton-upon-Trent brewing industry was primarily dependent upon the export of dark, sweet, very strong beer to Baltic ports including Prussia, Poland, Sweden, Russia, and the German Confederation.[51] Unlike the porter brewers who were concentrated around London, Burton-upon-Trent did not have a strong local consumer population so when the export trade to the Baltics effectively collapsed in 1822, brewers including Bass and Allsopp switched to producing pale and bright, or clear, beers for East Indies consumers in competition with the larger brewers of London.[52] However, there was consistent criticism of the export beers sent from Great Britain, specifically that the beers had "too much alcohol, too much sediment, too much hops and too little gas."[53] These critiques would continue regularly in the press and colonial reports through the end of the nineteenth century.

Foreign trade to India was difficult, with only the strongest beers able to survive in enough good shape for sale after the journey to Calcutta, Bombay, and Madras. Not only was it hard for the beer itself to arrive in a palatable state, but the amount of time between placing and receiving orders of ale was very long. The chance of loss was very high and in the intervening time between the order and fulfillment of it, commercial conditions and pricing sometimes changed for the worse. This meant limited shipments for commercial sale.[54] Yet even though beer exports were modest, they were unceasing. With the official naval ration of a gallon of beer a day per man, "afloat, as ashore, beer was the national drink."[55]

Another reason for the decline of exports was the diffusion of the brewing skills in the British brewing industry. When British brewers moved to breweries in export destinations, beer trade with the metropole often closed as soon as local breweries produced enough beer for the area. This was true of locations around the Baltic Sea, including St. Petersburg, Russia and Gothenburg, Sweden. When porter breweries were established in 1822 and 1826, respectively, it meant the end of English imports.[56]

---

[51] Mathias, *The Brewing Industry in England, 1700–1830*, 171, 176.
[52] Gourvish and Wilson, *The British Brewing Industry, 1830–1980*, 90.
[53] "Our Export Trade in Beer," *Brewers' Journal*, 2/15/90, 64.
[54] Mathias, *The Brewing Industry in England, 1700–1830*, 189.
[55] Mathias, *The Brewing Industry in England, 1700–1830*, 196.
[56] Mathias, *The Brewing Industry in England, 1700–1830*, 186.

Closer to home, the Irish beer trade throughout the eighteenth century was made up of English imports. This changed in the early nineteenth century as the Irish brewing industry grew around the production from the Guinness family at the St. James's Gate Brewery in Dublin. Unlike in England, there was no push toward a tied house trade in Ireland, and instead Irish brewers, including Guinness, focused on export. By 1840, over half of Guinness' annual production of 80,000 barrels were sold in England.[57] Guinness was very similar to Burton-upon-Trent's brewing firms, including Bass, in that it concentrated much of its production for export not to colonies but to English urban centers like London. This lack of interest in building new foreign markets would continue through the nineteenth century. Thus, even though Britain and Ireland were known for the quality of their beer, the business strategies of the brewing firms remained focused on domestic markets and the competition with other national breweries.

Toward the end of the 1860s, in spite of a decline in the export trade, the commentators for the British *Brewers' Journal* were very optimistic in the future of beer exports from Great Britain. They noted that trade would likely "extend in scale," and that "brewing is being conducted on an increasing basis annually."[58] Furthermore, they claimed that British beer was being introduced in new locations all over the world and that "England will always hold her own in that in which she has achieved such great results for ages past, and that in every part of the habitable globe English beer is, and will be, drunk in preference to the brewing of any other country."[59] The commentators' optimism, however, would not halt the rapid spread in the popularity of pilsner over the coming years.

Between 1830 and 1870, British brewers were united in their insular focus on domestic markets. However, opinions over how to brew varied considerably between the thousands of brewers in the UK. What would occur in brewing industries across the world began in England with a divide between operative/traditional brewers and practical/scientific brewers. Debates over how to brew beer continued throughout the nineteenth century over whether to brew beer

---

[57] Mathias, *The Brewing Industry in England, 1700–1830*, 167.
[58] "Board of Trade Returns," *Brewers' Journal*, 1/15/1868.
[59] "Board of Trade Returns."

based upon traditional tried-and-true methods or to change procedures based on new scientific evidence and using new technologies. The British brewing industry was, to its detriment, consistently slow to incorporate new science and technology over the course of the nineteenth century after the initial push of industrialization of British brewing between 1750 and 1830. By the 1830s, the industry had settled on a uniformity of practice based on scientific explanations but changed little over the next sixty years.[60]

Part II: Germany and Pilsner

Brewing in the German lands for most of the last millennium consisted of top-fermented beer produced in a similar way to beers in Great Britain.[61] However, by the eighteenth-century brown lager beers were popular enough in Bavaria to push top-fermented wheat beer out of most of the market. The popularity of lager beers was slow until the 1830s when brewers in Bavaria and then other German regions began producing them regularly. Their popularity then began to spread abroad in the 1840s.[62] When compared with the British brewing industry in the early nineteenth century, the Northern and Southern German brewers were far behind in terms of science, technology, and business acumen. However, by the end of the century German brewers and the styles of beer they produced were positioned to dominate brewing markets around the globe.

Foundation of Lager Brewing

Benno Scharl was arguably the founder of modern lager brewing techniques. *Beschreibung der Braunbier-Brauery im Koenigreiche Baiern* (Description of a Brown Beer Brewery in the Kingdom of Bavaria), published in Munich in 1814, introduced the cold aging of beer in Bavaria, emphasizing the need for temperature control during lagering. Scharl wrote that

---

[60] Gourvish and Wilson, *The British Brewing Industry, 1830–1980*, 47.
[61] Teich, *Bier, Wissenschaft und Wirtschaft in Deutschland 1800–1914*, 24.
[62] Teich, *Bier, Wissenschaft und Wirtschaft in Deutschland 1800–1914*, 26.

Warmth is of greater harm for lager beer (*Lagerbier*) than coldness ... If one cannot remain at a temperature of only eight degrees above the freezing-point ... the bottom ferment (*Unterzeug-Gaehrungsmittel*) cannot be used anymore. Contrary to the top ferment (*Spund-Gaehrung*)—used for brewing barley and wheat beer—[that] still can be used due to its greater durability during warmth.[63]

While the pilsner-style itself originated in Plzen, Bohemia, it was German brewers and businessmen who catapulted the golden lager and bottom fermented beer in general to a place of global recognition and domination through the adoption of technology, scientific knowledge, and federal and private investment. However, the brewing industry did not reach a place of competition with the British until the last quarter of the nineteenth century. The following section explores the state of the German brewing industry between 1750 and 1870 in order to highlight the connections between the Continental industrialization of the brewing industry and the industrialized British brewing industry.

The Sedlmayrs and the Spaten Brewery, Munich, Bavaria

While the British brewing industry was industrializing and innovating through the late eighteenth century, the brewing industries in Denmark, Northern and Central Germany had all "greatly retrograded" through ruinous trade and harmful tariffs. Imported wines and schnapps had caught the public's attention as their perception of the quality of beer had declined.[64] However, in Southern Germany, extra care was given to storing beer in ice cellars (*felsen kellern*). The methods of brewing in Bavaria were "perpetuated and improved upon" and by the 1880s were "adopted in the best breweries in most countries in Europe and elsewhere, as throughout North America."[65] According to J. C. Jacobsen of Carlsberg Brewery in 1884, the Continental brewing industries were defective through the 1830s. This was because the work was entirely "rule-of-thumb"

---

[63] Benno Scharl, *Beschreibung der Braunbier-Brauery im Koenigreiche Baiern* (Munich, 1814), Part V. Trans. Michael Jackson: MJ/4/17/45 Modern Sedlmayr Project I.
[64] J. C. Jacobsen, "Brewing Progress during the Last Fifty Years," *Brewers' Journal*, 1/15/1885, 30.
[65] Jacobsen, "Brewing Progress during the Last Fifty Years," 30.

without a trace of theoretical knowledge and "guided by tradition handed down from generation to generation,"[66] in same manner as the British brewing industry, instead of through formal education.

Breweries on the Continent in the early nineteenth century were usually located in small, crowded neighborhoods that made it impossible to maintain cleanliness. Brewery production was imperfect with all the work done by hand, making it expensive, hard work that could lead to poor beer quality.[67] However, brewing took a positive turn due to the travels of Gabriel Sedlmayr of Munich and Anton Dreher of Vienna in the mid-1830s.

The Spaten Brewery, founded in 1397, was bought by Gabriel Sedlmayr (Elder) in 1807 and was the smallest of Munich's fifty-two breweries (440HL/year) at the beginning of the nineteenth century. Gabriel's two sons, Josef and Gabriel (Younger) apprenticed in the brewery beginning in 1825. The apprenticeship for Bavarian brewers, however, not only included instruction about brewing in their own brewery and running the business but also included "wandering years" in and outside of Bavaria to learn different brewing techniques and approaches. Josef and Gabriel (Younger), as well as their companion Anton Dreher of the Schwechat Brewery located just outside Vienna, set out on an extensive journey through other parts of Germany, Austria, Bohemia, Belgium, Holland, and, most importantly, Scotland and England.[68]

Between July 25 and December 31, 1833, the two Sedlmayrs and Dreher visited breweries in Scotland and England including those in Birmingham, Manchester, Liverpool, Glasgow, Alloa, Dundee, Montrose, Edinburgh, Newcastle, Sheffield, and Burton-upon-Trent. In these locations, they met with maltsters and brewers to learn the newest malting and brewing techniques and bring them back to the Continent.[69] The British brewers proved to be civil but secretive when dealing with the visitors and only provided them with broad insight into the methods they used rather than the practical understanding

---

[66] Jacobsen, "Brewing Progress during the Last Fifty Years," 30.
[67] Jacobsen, "Brewing Progress during the Last Fifty Years," 30.
[68] Michael Jackson: MJ/4/17/45 Modern Sedlmayr Project I, 70–1.
[69] Brock, *Dreihundert Jarhre Brauhaus Schwechat* (Wein: Selbst-verlag der Vereinigten Brauereien AG, 1932), 32–3. MJ/4/17/45.

of technical and economic skills. The visitors resorted to industrial espionage to gain the knowledge they desired and used secret thermometers and saccharometers, which they had only just learned the existence of, while also surreptitiously looking at their hosts' brewery notes. They created hollow metal poles with valves on the bottom, which they painted to look like wooden walking canes, in order to procure samples of wort and beer to test later with saccharometers.[70] In this way the wandering apprentices were able to gain the knowledge and skills of the British brewers and transport the information home to Austria and Bavaria.

As we know, British brewers at this point were far ahead of Continental brewers in terms of brewing knowledge and technology. Sedlmayr and the others soon learned about the use of a thermometer to determine temperature during steeping, germination, kilning, brewing, wort cooling and fermentation. In addition, they learned of the benefits of the saccharometer in figuring out the actual and potential strength of their beer. Though Sedlmayr went on to confirm for Continental brewers the advantages of bottom-fermentation versus top-fermentation due to the latter being more prone to "beer vermins" like wild yeast and bacteria, the process of malting in England was very different in comparison with Central Europe and provided an excellent method to create lightly colored, quality malt. Part of this process, also known in England, allowed for the retention of enzyme strength in the malt through the pre-drying of green malt in kilns.[71]

Technology on the Continent

Prior to the apprentices' journeys to the UK, scientific knowledge in brewing on the Continent was limited. However, some work had been done that would have important consequences for brewing industries there. In 1833, Anselme Payen and Jean-François Persoz discovered the enzyme diastase that converted starch into sugar for fermentation. The original belief had been that the conversion of starch to sugar and dextrin took place in malting and the mashing that followed only brought them into the solution of liquid.

---

[70] Brock, *Dreihundert Jarhre Brauhaus,* 71–2.
[71] Brock, *Dreihundert Jarhre Brauhaus,* 32–3. MJ/4/17/45.

Their pioneering work showed that the preparation for this transformation took place during mashing when the "diastatic ferment" developed during germination. This meant that proper mashing was perhaps the most important process for brewers and needed special care for precise temperature controls.[72]

The discovery of diastase and the importance of mashing in the brewing process created a need for precision that Continental brewers had not realized. For instance, the use of a thermometer, brought from Britain by the Sedlemayrs and Dreher, was rare until the discoveries about the necessity for temperature precision were understood in regard to malting, mashing, and fermentation. Precision to tenths of a degree meant that brewers needed the tools introduced from Britain to produce better quality beer. In addition, prior to the travels of the apprentices, the saccharometer only existed in the British Isles and the strength of beer was estimated by the volume brewed from a certain quantity of malt. Brewers used "beer-tasters" to decide if the beer was "*ein ehrlicher trunk*" or "*pfenning vergultig*" (an "honest drink" or "only worth a penny").[73] The problem with this was that malt quality and sugar content varied considerably, which led to broad variations in beer strength and a lack of quality assurance. When Sedlmayr and Dreher returned, they brought with them the knowledge of how to use saccharometers to determine the strength and yield of their malted grain. They were able to purchase their own saccharometer in Berlin and were the first to use one for brewing in Munich—and in all of Germany—on May 6, 1834.[74,75]

In addition to scientific tools, Sedlmayr and Dreher brought back knowledge about the value of suitable brewing machinery, which resulted in the introduction of steam power and machinery in South Germany and Austrian breweries.[76] They also brought back new methods for treating grain during malting, including the benefits of slower germination for a higher sugar concentration for the wort and how to malt barley for lighter-colored beers.

---

[72] Jacobsen, "Brewing Progress during the Last Fifty Years," 108.

[73] Jacobsen, "Brewing Progress during the Last Fifty Years," 108. German translation by Jennifer Roesch.

[74] Brock, *Dreihundert Jarhre Brauhaus*, 71.

[75] In 1839, Gabriel and Josef took over the Spaten Brewery after their father died. In 1842, however, Gabriel took over after Josef sold him his shares of the brewery in order to buy his own, Leistbrauerai.

[76] Jacobsen, "Brewing Progress during the Last Fifty Years," 30.

It took time for other brewers to start incorporating the skills brought back by the Sedlmayr and Dreher. This was partially due to the fact that at first, they were not willing to share with others until they established themselves as central figures in the Munich and Vienna brewing scenes. In addition, most other brewers were not interested in the use of saccharometers during the brewing process, only caring about the finished beer's strength and quality, though they usually did not even try to brew beers of consistent strength.[77] The introduction of the saccharometer via the British represents the beginning of the scientific brewing in Germany but even though there was widespread interest in reliable testing of beer early in the nineteenth century, it did not happen until after 1845 outside of Spaten and a few other breweries.[78]

In addition to Sedlmayr and Dreher's contributions, another important event occurred in German brewing with the publishing of the German translation of the British Parliamentary Report from 1806 regarding tax rates related to malted grain using saccharometers. This led to the development of the Balling saccharometer by Carl Joseph Napoleon Balling, a professor of general and applied technical chemistry at the polytechnic school in Prague. Through the British report, Balling learned of attenuation and specific gravities in the brewing process and started a series of over a hundred experiments in fermentation that helped him develop his own saccharometer and to publish *Die sacharometrische Probe* in 1845. While only fifty pages long, this piece was a milestone in the development of the scientific treatment of fermentation in Continental Europe.[79]

Anton Dreher and Schwechat Brewery

It took some time for bottom-fermented beer to rise in popularity in Central Europe. Though Scharl's work influenced brewers in Bavaria, in Vienna Anton Dreher continued to brew top fermented beer through the 1830s. His most popular style was "Kaiserbier," a top-fermented, mild, and "drinkable" (*seuffiges*) beer.[80]

---

[77] Brock, *Dreihundert Jarhre Brauhaus*, 69–70.
[78] Brock, *Dreihundert Jarhre Brauhaus*, 58.
[79] Brock, *Dreihundert Jarhre Brauhaus*, 83–4.
[80] Brock, *Dreihundert Jarhre Brauhaus*, 29. Trans. Michael Jackson: MJ/4/17/45 Modern Sedlmayr Project I.

In the 1840s, while most beer drinkers in Austria were accustomed to inferior quality ales, Bavarian-produced lagers were gaining traction in the region via shipping networks. In 1841, only Dreher's rival, the Huetteldorfer Brewery, had introduced domestic lager production of "Maerzen" beer in small quantities at high prices, which he attempted to compete with through his "Kaiserbier." In the winter of 1840 Dreher's master brewer, Johann Goetz, began brewing his own bottom-fermented beer and, after fermentation, delivered it immediately to proprietors who had to store the beer before it could be sold to the public. However, after Dreher's "Klein Schwachater Lagerbier" was introduced to the public it was enthusiastically welcomed in Vienna.[81]

Pilsner: The First Golden Lager

In February 1838, a representative of the Austrian Empire arrived from Vienna to test the drinkability of the local beer in the Bohemian city of Pilsen. Unfortunately, the testing showed that the beer produced at the time was not fit to be consumed and so all thirty-six barrels of beer on hand were poured into the sewer in front of the town hall, much to the consternation of the local burghers. In response, the town Burghers petitioned the city to produce quality beer for the local population. As Vaclav Mirwald, the holder and publican of "U zlateho oral" said, "This is necessary to us in Pilsen—good and cheep [sic] beer!"[82]

On January 2, 1839, the town burghers who held brewing privileges sent out a declaration to construct a city-owned brewery and malthouse called the Citizens' Brewery (or Burghers' Brewery).[83] To this end, they hired an architect, Martin Stelzer, to tour Europe in order to learn of the latest and best technology and methods for producing beer. Stelzer returned in spring 1842 with knowledge, a building plan, and a brewer named Josef Groll from Bavaria to begin production of a new state-of-the-art brewery in Pilsen. Groll was known as a simple man without any proper manners and, according to

---

[81] Brock, *Dreihundert Jarhre Brauhaus*, 32–3. MJ/4/17/45.
[82] *Pilsner Urquell: Plzensky Prazdroj N.P. Plzen 1842–1982* (Czechoslovakia: publisher not identified), Chapter 3.
[83] *Pilsner Urquell.*

his father, was the rudest man in Bavaria.[84] However, he had an excellent reputation as a brewer and supervised the building of the new brewery that was completed in September 1842. The first batch of beer, using local barley grain and Saaz hops, began brewing October 5, 1842, and was completed November 11 with the first pilsner lager poured at the St. Martin's Market.

Groll's beer combined lager brewing techniques developed by Sedlmayr at Spaten in Munich with the malting technology from England and brought to Bavaria by the Sedlmayr brothers and Dreher to create the pilsner. Within the first year of production the Citizens' Brewery produced 6,326 hogsheads of beer (12,652 Barrels) and shipped a good part of it to Prague. The popularity of the new pilsner-style caught on quickly, and by 1852 there were already controversies over the name of "pilsner," enough so that the Citizens' Brewery published in Prague newspapers to combat the theft of the name and style. The brewery owners beseeched pilsner consumers by asking:

> In the effort to put an end to practicing on non-resident consumers and perverting the sale of fake beer, we inform everybody who would like to buy genuine pilsner beer made by bottom-fermentation that the sale of this beer in transport barrels is exclusively provided by the administration of the Citizens' Brewery in Pilsen, who include the certificate of delivery with each supply. Therefore we beg you to turn to them only.[85]

Unfortunately for the Citizens' Brewery, even as they expanded their production and modernized over the coming decades, the golden lager style known as pilsner, which literally translates as "from Pilsen," spread beyond their control.

Business

On October 1, 1866, the growing popularity of the beer trade led to the abolishment of all restrictions to the sale of beer in the kingdom of Bavaria. Brewers decided together to sell beer at the same moderate price in summer and winter with a standardized serving measure that was stamped by the

---

[84] Eduard Jalowetz, Ivo Hlaváček, and Jindřiška Eliášková, *Pilsner Beer in the Light of Practice and Science* (Plzeň: Euroverlag, 2001).

[85] Jalowetz, et. al., *Pilsner Beer in the Light of Practice and Science*.

authorities.[86] The reasons for this were to benefit both the brewers and the government. The government was now able to regulate beer sales easier through standardized measures and was able to do so without dealing with local differences. The brewers benefited by no longer having any restrictions on selling their products across a broader region with unfettered access to more markets.

Brewery companies around Germany began producing lager beers quickly during the 1860s as the popularity of pilsners/Bavarian bottom-fermented beers spread rapidly. In 1866, the Brewery Company at Bergedorf began selling its own "Bavarian imitation beer" and immediately enjoyed "great popularity among the beer-drinkers at Hamburg, in spite of great competition" in the city.[87] Breweries founded in Berlin also utilized the popular name of Bavaria. New breweries like the "Bavaria" brewery company held little risk for investors according to brewing industry literature. "Beer—and especially good beer—is always in demand, being no longer an article of luxury, but of imperative necessity in every large city."[88] Except in a few cases the market for lager continued to grow with new breweries and brewing companies becoming regularly established in Germany and abroad.

Though British breweries did not begin incorporating until the late 1880s, Continental breweries were quick to utilize this business tactic decades earlier in order to raise investment for expensive lager breweries. Sale of the popular pilsner lagers, also known as Bavarian lagers, was rapidly increasing through the 1860s with lager breweries established outside of Germany in cities like St. Petersburg where the "Bavaria Joint Stock Brewery" was selling over 230,000 gallons of lager in its first six months.[89] The growing popularity did not go unnoticed by the British government either.

In a series of reports before Parliament in 1866, British foreign ministers noted that the manufacture and consumption of beer in Bavaria had nearly doubled in the previous fifteen years with demand continuing to increase. In Munich, breweries continued to grow in scale with the trade accumulating in

---

[86] "Bavarian Beer," *Brewers' Journal*, 9/15/1865, 22.
[87] "Opening of the Bergedorf Brewery," *Brewers' Journal*, 2/17/1866, 10.
[88] "The 'Bavaria' New Brewery Company at Berlin," *Brewers' Journal*, 11/17/1866, 121–2.
[89] "The St. Petersburg Brewery 'Bavaria,'" *Brewers' Journal*, 2/17/1866, 10.

the "hands of a few considerable capitalists." While the number of breweries had declined, the amount of beer produced continued to grow due to public and private investment through incorporation.[90]

The consolidation of breweries was not limited to Bavaria and Germany. In Austria, there was a "great revolution in beer production" between 1846 and 1866. While there was a decrease of about 200 breweries, there was a "large increase in their aggregate production."[91] Smaller breweries gave up and larger establishments "with more extensive capital, the most modern improvements in the machinery and art of brewing, and a greater degree of energy and intelligence," absorbed their business.[92]

Exports

Early on, lager brewers in Germany looked to export markets. The Hamburg Joint-Stock Company had its first general meeting of shareholders in 1866. At this meeting the new directors proposed to increase the capital in order to extend to foreign countries. Though the shareholders did not support this proposal, it does show that brewery company managers were immediately looking to expand their reach beyond local markets.[93] This included the brewery of Anton Dreher as well. By 1868, Dreher sent weekly railway ice-wagons filled with lager to Amsterdam for immediate consumption. However, by that time Dreher's lager beer had a "formidable competitor in the 'Nederlandsch Beyersch Bierbrouwery'" that had recently completed construction.[94] Austrian beer also made it to London by the following year though it was met with derision by the local press.[95]

Though the British press continued to point out a steady progression of British beer exports to the "open markets of the world," the focus of the brewers themselves was on their domestic markets and maintaining assured

---

[90] "Foreign Hops, Beer, Wine, &c.," *Brewers' Journal*, 5/19/1866, 54.
[91] "The Beer Trade in Austria," *Brewers' Journal*, 10/20/1866, 116.
[92] "The Beer Trade in Austria," 116.
[93] "The Hamburg Joint-Stock Company," *Brewers' Journal*, 2/17/1866, 10.
[94] "Items of Continental News," *Brewers' Journal*, 6/15/1868, 92.
[95] "The Export of British and Import of German Beer," *Brewers' Journal*, 4/15/1869, 65.

profits through tied houses.[96] German companies, on the other hand, were already looking beyond their local markets toward foreign opportunities for sales.

Conclusion

The British brewing industry through the 1860s was ahead of the rest of the world in technology and business acumen in comparison to Continental brewing industries. Yet, it also had latent flaws that would come back to haunt the industry after the rise of global competition. Through corporate espionage and the diffusion of technology in the 1830s, brewers in Bavaria and the surrounding regions were able to begin the process of transitioning from decidedly pre-industrial brewing production processes to industrial brewing that would incorporate the latest scientific and technological innovations. The beer that would help this transition through its popularity at home and abroad was the pilsner, the first golden lager.

Without the scientific and technological advances made by the British brewing industry, Continental brewing would not have been able to develop as quickly as it did during the middle of the nineteenth century. By adopting the production methods of the British and then adding their own innovations, the Continental brewers were able to establish their own competitive breweries across Europe. However, the differences in their approaches to education, science, and financial investment diverged dramatically from the British as the century continued on.

By 1889, the popularity of pilsner was even evident to a British court. The Imperial and Royal Austro-Hungarian Consulate-General in London brought the matter of the term "Pilsener Bier" to the attention of the General Customs Office in London due to a disagreement regarding lager beer imported to England from Germany (mainly Hamburg and Bremen) under the name of Pilsener. The Consulate-General sought changes in this labeling on the basis of the provisions of the Merchandise Marks Act of 1887 in which descriptions of goods, under which all incorrect and misleading designations of goods

---

[96] "The Export of British and Import of German Beer," 65.

in relation to type, quantity, place of manufacture and the like are strictly prohibited. However, the Customs Office ruled that the name pilsner was understood in London to be a particular style of beer outside of a "particular place of production, so that the use of that designation is not contrary to English law, at least in cases in which it appears supplemented by an additional statement referring to the actual provenance, such as 'made in Bremen.'"[97] The pilsner had officially lost its connection to its geographic origin as the beer's popularity transformed global beer production and consumption.

---

[97] Peter Dyer, "'Pilsener Beer' in London in 1891," *Brewery History*, (117), 2004, 36–9.

2

Modern Methods: European Brewing Technology and Science

Introduction

Between 1870 and 1914, technological and scientific advances changed many of the processes of brewing beer. These innovations included the expanded use of steam power in the brewery and in transportation, the development and incorporation of mechanized refrigeration, and the use of scientific knowledge including the biology of fermentation and the chemistry of malt conversion in the brewing process. However, the responses and acceptance of these changes varied depending on where one was a brewer. The German and other Continental brewers accepted these changes quickly and readily for the most part. The British brewers, on the other hand, were slow to make use of these innovations. These specific, differing, choices by the different national European brewing industries were very important in the British decline as the premier beer brewing power in the world by the late 1880s. By examining the different approaches to the adoption of the latest science and technology, we can see how and why Continental brewers were able to surpass British breweries in the quality and distribution of their beer by the end of the nineteenth century.

Science and technology are very important for brewing good quality beer. Though the basic processes of making beer (malting, mashing, boiling, cooling, and fermentation) have remained largely unchanged throughout history, the industrialization of the brewing process in Europe made these processes faster, far more efficient, and more cost-effective. These advances allowed brewers to produce beers that were consistent in strength and taste and with better shelf lives so the beer could last longer before consumption, allowing it travel much farther in better condition. Just as the use of hops in the twelfth and thirteenth centuries led to the development of beer export trades in northern Europe due to the preservative qualities of the hop flowers, the development of temperature controls, pasteurization, and better modes of transportation led to another revolution in the possibilities of beer exportation both within and outside of Europe.[1]

The inclusion of the natural sciences to the brewing industry created sharp divides between "scientific" brewers who used the scientific knowledge to their advantage and "practical" brewers who used traditional brewing methods with little understanding of microbiology and chemistry. For the most part, scientific brewing was a Continental choice while the majority of British brewers followed tradition. While some brewers, especially the British, sought to maintain what they saw as traditional brewing practices, many other brewers were quick to include scientists and scientific knowledge in their breweries with the goal of consistent, high-quality beer. Between 1870 and 1914, the beer—mostly golden lagers—produced by scientific brewers came to dominate the beer markets due to their more consistent products, longer shelf lives, and the public perception of quality regarding the product.

Compared with lager production in Germany, the British ale fermentation systems were idiosyncratic and varied considerably between breweries. Due to a general lack of interest in scientific advances as well as a lack of collaboration between brewers, the production of British beer occurred at temperatures barely within the safety margin for decent quality during mashing and fermentation through the 1880s in both the large urban breweries and the smaller country brewers.[2] Continental brewers, on the other hand, brewed their beer utilizing specific temperature controls based upon exact specifications developed through scientific methods.

The British brewers were not eager for new technology and scientific advances in part because they lacked an economic need to do so due to strong domestic markets for the beers they produced using traditional methods. They produced the styles of beer the British consumer wanted, which by the 1880s were full-flavored, strong, and pale.[3] The production of strong ales, porters, and

---

[1] For more on the spread of hops see Richard W. Unger, *Beer in the Middle Ages and the Renaissance* (Philadelphia: University of Pennsylvania Press, 2004).

[2] T. R. Gourvish and R. G. Wilson, *The British Brewing Industry, 1830–1980* (New York: Cambridge University Press, 1994), 58.

[3] Gourvish and Wilson, *The British Brewing Industry*, 58.

stouts had few problems outside of production during the hottest months of the year when temperature control was difficult and could lead to poor quality beer. The production of light ales remained a constant problem even after the 1880s when scientific advances such as "pure yeast" would have made it much easier.

Overall, ale brewing in Great Britain was much cheaper than lager brewing. Lager brewing required large quantities of ice in summer, large cellars for aging the beer in cold temperatures, and entailed a much slower turnover of capital.[4] The lager brewers required an enormous investment in education and the purchase of equipment for bottom-fermentation, ice for temperature control, and storage systems for ice and aging their beer (*lagering*). In addition, even with the introduction of ice machines in the 1870s, brewing took about four months for a finished batch of lager, in comparison with about four weeks for the popular "running ales" in Great Britain.[5]

This chapter examines the different scientific and technological approaches taken by British and Continental brewers. I argue that the spread and popularity of pilsners, in comparison to British beer styles, occurred in part because the British did not adopt a modern scientific approach to brewing while the Continental brewers did. Through their continued attempts to improve their brewing methods through scientific collaboration using the latest technology, Continental brewers produced beer that was superior to that of the British. Though British brewers eventually adopted many of the advances that made pilsner popular and of higher quality, they did so slowly and unevenly across the industry while continuing to produce beers that few outside the UK wanted to drink.

Part I: Technology

Transportation

Steam technology significantly affected the transportation of beer as it did for many consumer goods. First railroads and then steam ships came to be used in the transportation of beer both to domestic markets and then international

---

[4] Gourvish and Wilson, *The British Brewing Industry*, 58.
[5] Gourvish and Wilson, *The British Brewing Industry*, 176.

and colonial markets. The greater speed with which beer could be sent around the world made for a better quality of product in export markets regardless of beer style. However, the rapid transportation also made it possible for those with better access and motivation to take over markets that others may have controlled. In Bavaria, small-time brewers were barely making ends meet until opportunities for export arrived with railroads and steamers. Though Bavarian brewers initially exported to other German states, they soon found markets for their lagers all over Europe. The great exhibitions of the middle and late nineteenth century provided occasions for introducing their beer to new consumers in markets all over Europe that helped promote the spread of golden lagers over ales in markets within the continent and beyond.[6]

The transportation of beer via steam ships had several obstacles to overcome. In comparison to spirits, beer takes up more space for less profit. Though shipping companies knew that the product would sell, it also took up a lot of space that could be used for items that were more expensive. Also, before the development and utilization of pasteurization many kinds of beer would spoil during the journey abroad. The continuous jostling and temperature changes that could occur with overseas travel would frequently lead to spoiled beer, or at the very least, an inconsistent article upon arrival. The changes of the later nineteenth century, including faster and more stable steam ships, made it possible for beer to arrive in better and more consistent shape than ever before.

Railroads

Railroads were an important part of transporting beer both in Great Britain and on the Continent. In England, the expansion of railroads was slow through the early nineteenth century but occurred rapidly through the 1840s and 1850s. Beer distribution nationwide became cheap and fast with reduced freight charges that changed the market strategy for brewers in Burton and London, especially after 1839 when Burton linked to London. With the journey time from Burton to London dropping from three weeks to only twelve hours, new domestic markets become more viable for trade.[7]

---

[6] Regarding excitement over the selection of Continental lager beers at the Paris Exhibition in 1878: "Observations on the Analysis of Austrian, Bavarian, and Bohemian Beer," *Country Brewers' Gazette* (Yorkshire, England), Vol. 2, 5/13/1878, 224.

[7] Gourvish and Wilson, *The British Brewing Industry*, 150.

Railroads also allowed for the creation of agencies and stores that became the central distribution network of beer for breweries such as Bass, from Burton, after 1840. In the 1850s, there was even a limited push for beer exports due to the popularity of Burton pale ales, early expansion of railroads, and the Great Exhibition.[8] The Great Exhibition, like later national exhibitions, brought people and exhibits from all over Europe and showcased national goods including locally produced beers.[9]

Steamships

While railroads had a great impact from the early nineteenth century, with freight rates declining from 1815 onward, the impact of steam ships was not felt until the last third of the century.[10] In 1880, three times as much waterborne freight was transported by sailing ships than by steam. However, with the help of coal mining, steam power spread quickly over the course of the decade. Steel ships, the compound engine, and the surface condenser all supported the transition from sail to steam between 1880 and 1914 with the British merchant marine securing almost half of the world's carrying power by 1888.[11] Through these technological inventions as well institutional innovations, commodity freight rates dropped for the busiest oceanic routes due to fierce competition between shipping companies. Governments subsidized many of these companies so they could transport mail, colonial officials, and supplies, and maintain merchant marine fleets.[12] For instance, the German shipping lines that served East Africa were heavily subsidized by the German government, which would offer rebates to shippers who fulfilled their annual tonnage quota. In order to be sure they received their rebate and met the required tonnage, many would top up their tonnage with whiskey and beer for colonists.[13]

---

[8] Gourvish and Wilson, *The British Brewing Industry*, 172–3.
[9] M. Vogel, "The Beer Trade of the World," *Brewers' Journal*, 9/15/1884, 332.
[10] Steven Topik and Allen Wells, "Commodity Chains in a Global Economy," in *A World Connecting*, ed. Emily S. Rosenberg (Cambridge, MA: Belknap Press of Harvard University Press, 2012), 630.
[11] Topik and Wells, "Commodity Chains in a Global Economy," 634.
[12] Topik and Wells, "Commodity Chains in a Global Economy," 631–2.
[13] "Africa," National Brewing Library (Oxford Brooks University, Oxford, England), MJ/4/40/1.

Through steamships the nature of freight changed due to the amount of goods the large ships could carry. Sailing freights usually carried luxury items that would be cost-effective and take up as little space as possible. With the advent of large steamships, bulk commodities that had a high volume-to-value ratio, such as coal, meat, grains, and tropical goods, all became the most important. Since travel times were more certain with steam, easily spoiled goods could be transported successfully across the oceans.[14]

The primary motivations for the shipping revolution in steam were imperial and commercial. The domination of the seas was a continuing goal for Great Britain and then for the United States and Germany. The rivalry between Germany and Britain accelerated naval building by both countries through the turn of the twentieth century.[15]

As railroads in Britain cut down domestic transport times significantly, steamships did the same across the world. For instance, in 1840 it took six weeks to sail from England to Calcutta, but by 1914 it only took twelve days with the help of steam power and the Suez Canal. The journey to Australia dropped from 125 days in the early nineteenth century to a month by 1900 and a steamship voyage from the United States to Europe went from nine or ten days to five or six days.[16]

Steam-Powered Machines

Brewers in the late eighteenth century were already utilizing the power of steam engines for several processes in their breweries, especially in pumping water, wort, and beer around the breweries at different stages of the brewing process through the use of Watts steam engine, which made complicated, steam-operated machinery possible for use during the brewing process while also reducing transportation costs.[17] Steam power was also quickly utilized in other stages including the crushing of malted grains before mashing. Over the course of the nineteenth century, steam power came to be used for many more processes in beer production.

---

[14] Topik and Wells, "Commodity Chains in a Global Economy," 633.
[15] Topik and Wells, "Commodity Chains in a Global Economy," 635.
[16] Topik and Wells, "Commodity Chains in a Global Economy," 637–8.
[17] Johan F. M. Swinnen, *The Economics of Beer* (New York: Oxford University Press, 2011), 15.

Figure 2.1 Pilsen Brewhouse.

In 1865, German brewers were only using steam power very modestly and usually all a brewery really needed was a stationary engine of around 12hp for pumping liquid. This continued through the 1870s and early 1880s because most of their work was done by hand, aside from pumping and driving elevators.[18] But even this was notable at the Exhibition of Vienna in 1873 where the great strides of Germany were highlighted. Steam power was shown to be in more general use, especially with machinery in the new brewery buildings. In contrast to Continental progress, ale production in Britain saw very little improvement.[19] However, over the course of the 1880s there came a reduction in the number

---

[18] Mikulas Teich, "The Industrialization of Brewing in Germany (1800–1914)," in *Production, Marketing, and Consumption of Alcoholic Beverages since the Late Middle Ages: Session B-14: Proceedings, Tenth International Economic History Congress, Leuven, August 1990*, eds. International Economic History Congress, Aerts Erik Cullen L. M. Wilson R. G. (Leuven, Belgium, 1990), 106.

[19] Karl Lintner, "Recent Progress in the Art of Brewing in Germany," *Country Brewers' Gazette*, (Yorkshire, England), Vol. 2, 5/13/1878, 226.

of breweries as the preference for smaller breweries shifted in favor of medium and large enterprises. Even as the number of smaller breweries dwindled, the number of employees in each German brewery doubled. Small breweries typically had around two people working while medium ones had about sixteen people. Large breweries, however, grew to include an average of 111.[20]

In J. C. Jacobsen's address to the Technical Association of Copenhagen in 1884, the owner of the Carlsberg Brewery emphasized how important the introduction of machine power and improved apparatus was to the brewing industry. Not only did it improve the quality of the beer itself, but it had already increased the productive capabilities of the brewery from one to four brewings a day due to more efficient cooling apparatuses that saved a great deal of time. In terms of malting the barley there was also an important change. By using a steam-powered pneumatic malting apparatus to keep the malting grains in motion as well as powerful ventilating machines, the maltsters were able to increase the depth of grain on the malting floor from a four-inch depth to two feet while using the same floor space. In addition, with cooling instruments, the malting season had increased from eight to ten months a year by 1884. Machine labor, as Jacobsen explains, was extensively introduced in the drying of the malt by providing the mechanical means to replace hand labor in turning the malt for even drying across the entire malting floor.[21]

The economic and technical aspects of steam power mechanization were two sides of the same process. Breweries without efficient steam power could not progress and compete. As large breweries flourished, they were the only ones that could afford to purchase and run the new steam-powered machines.[22] For instance, by 1878, the Schwechat Brewery of Anton Dreher near Vienna was able to produce 500,000 barrels of beer that combined water and steam engines of one hundred horsepower, with added production support from 250 draught oxen.[23]

---

[20] Teich, "The Industrialization of Brewing in Germany (1800–1914)," in *Production, Marketing, and Consumption of Alcoholic Beverages since the Late Middle Ages*, 107–8.

[21] J. C. Jacobsen, "Brewing Progress during the Last Fifty Years," *Brewers' Journal*, Vol. 20, 1/15/1885, 30–1.

[22] Teich, "The Industrialization of Brewing in Germany (1800–1914)," in *Production, Marketing, and Consumption of Alcoholic Beverages since the Late Middle Ages*, 108.

[23] "Dreher's Brewery," *Brewers' Journal*, Vol. 13, 12/9/1878, 584.

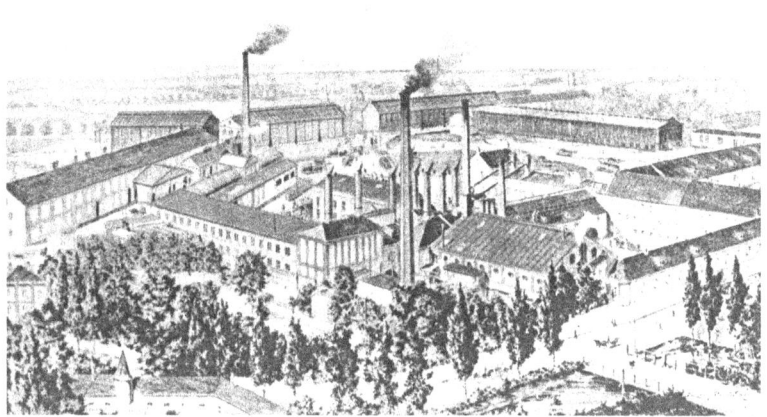

Figure 2.2 Schwechat Brewery Vienna.

Temperature Control in the Brewery

Temperature control has always been important in brewing beer. While the boiling portion of the process is the most simplistic once you have adequate fuel to raise the brewing liquor to the boiling point, temperature levels during malting and mashing, fermentation, and aging are very important to the finished product for ales and lagers. The following sections deal with changes in refrigeration technology that made it easier to produce lager beer by Continental brewers, helping them produce beer in greater quantities year-round, and at a higher quality, to the detriment of British ale brewers.

Temperature Control Background: Great Britain

With the invention and adoption of the thermometer at the end of the eighteenth century, British brewers were able to produce beer of a quality that no other brewers in the world could compete. While there were many different opinions about what temperatures were best for the different processes of brewing, within a few years nearly all the largest and most well-known brewers of Great Britain were using thermometers to regulate the temperature of all of their brewing processes. With the added knowledge that came from use of saccharometers to establish the correct density of the wort and strength of the finished beer the British brewers were producing more consistent beer than any other nation.

Used in tandem, thermometers and saccharometers allowed the brewers to produce wort with the most consistent amounts of fermentable sugars from the malted barley and control the fermentation of the wort into beer with consistency. As mentioned in Chapter 1, they also developed techniques for cooling the wort quickly from boiling to fermentation temperatures, which helped produce better and more consistent quality beer as well. These early temperature regulators made it possible for British brewers to do away with previous traditions that did not allow for beer brewing during the warmer months from April to October. However, the ales produced by the British needed less temperature regulation than the lagers produced on the Continent. To produce lager of a higher quality the brewers needed more space and different tools than British ale brewers.

Temperature Control Background: Germany

With the needs for cold fermentation temperatures and an even colder lagering temperature to produce quality pilsner beer, Continental lager brewers were at a severe disadvantage in comparison to the British. While the early processes of malting and mashing were similar to ale production, the lower fermentation temperatures needed for bottom-fermenting yeasts as well as the extended 3–6-month lagering time made lager beer production much more difficult. In addition, brewing was limited to cold months even with the use of the moderate temperature controls developed by the British.

Lager brewers needed more space for their beer production. While the London porter brewers utilized large vats for the aging of their beers, they did not need to focus on much temperature control outside of the earthen temperatures available under the main brewery production sites.[24] Lager brewers, however, needed near-freezing temperatures for the extended aging of their beers. Thus, brewery sites were usually located next to hillsides where breweries dug large caves packed with ice to keep the beer cold. In addition, the beer needed to stay cold through to consumption to keep it from spoilage, especially before the incorporation of pasteurization in the brewing and distribution processes. For instance, Viennese lagers had to be brewed, aged, and transported at cold temperatures before they were served to English drinkers at the Great Exhibition according to the *Brewers' Journal* in 1872.[25]

Ice Machines and Mechanized Refrigeration

There were several refrigeration systems invented during the third quarter of the nineteenth century, but brewers both in Britain and on the Continent were slow to incorporate them into their breweries. Brewers were worried that the chemicals used in mechanized refrigeration would spoil their product and lead to financial loss. For many years, refrigeration was very experimental as inventors attempted systems that involved different kinds of gas and designs to produce cold temperatures, regulate those temperatures, and produce ice regardless of the location and season.

One of the early attempts in the 1870s involved the use of ether, but it was short-lived as the potential for ammonia-based ice machines took over. The introduction of machines like those produced by Reece's Patent Ice Company (Limited) in London were impressive events. For instance, in October 1877 a demonstration of Reece's ammonia-based ice machine was attended by around eighty of the leading scientific men of the country as well as the Chinese ambassador who came to witness how Reece's machine was able to make seven times as much ice with a single ton of coal as an earlier ether machine.[26] The ether machine in question worked well but proved to be very costly.[27] The brewery of

---

[24] Peter Mathias, *The Brewing Industry in England, 1700–1830* (England: Cambridge University Press, 1959).
[25] "Vienna Beer in London," *Brewers' Journal*, Vol. 7, 7/15/1872, 197.
[26] "Ice Making By Machinery," *Country Brewers' Gazette*, Vol. 1, 10/29/1877, 94.
[27] Jacobsen, "Brewing Progress during the Last Fifty Years," 30.

Meux and Co. had recently installed a machine with the cooling power equivalent to twenty tons of ice per day. The correspondent of the Country Brewers' Gazette who attended the event himself noted that "it was evident to all present that the necessity no longer exists for importing Norwegian ice, and there can be no doubt that at the cheap rate at which these machines produce the ice, the manufacture much supersede the import, with all its costs of storing, waste, and heavy expense."[28]

The use of steam power scaled up quickly with the introduction of artificial refrigeration to the brewing process during the second half of the 1880s. Prior to this, breweries were dependent upon natural ice for cooling that required the equivalent of one horsepower per kilogram of malt. After the introduction and installation of artificial refrigeration only three to four horsepower was needed per 50 kg of malt.[29]

This was an important change considering the growing needs of Continental lager breweries like Spaten in Munich. Between 1846 and 1869, the ice required by the Spaten Brewery rose from 10 kg to 73 kg per hectoliter of sold beer due to the expanding production of lager beer at the time. This expanding market for Spaten's lager led to the lifting of seasonal restrictions on brewing and, after 1865, bottom-fermented beer was brewed year-round which meant the needs for controlled, cold temperatures were that much greater.[30] A British visitor to Germany in the fall of 1877 noted that in most German towns there were no ice-machines and natural ice arrived by carriage from the north. The visitor noted correctly that natural ice was an enormous expense for the large breweries and that "ice-making machines have in Germany a great chance of success."[31]

In Jacobsen's 1884 address about the changes in brewing over the previous fifty years, he noted the importance of ice cellars in the soundness and freshness of his lagers at Carlsberg and across the Continent. The later use of ice with the wort and beer both before and during fermentation allowed for further

---

[28] "Ice Making By Machinery," 94.

[29] Teich, "The Industrialization of Brewing in Germany (1800–1914)," in *Production, Marketing, and Consumption of Alcoholic Beverages since the Late Middle Ages*, 109.

[30] Teich, "The Industrialization of Brewing in Germany (1800–1914)," in *Production, Marketing, and Consumption of Alcoholic Beverages since the Late Middle Ages*, 110.

[31] "Miscellaneous—Ice," *Country Brewers' Gazette*, Vol. 1, 11/12/1877, 118.

temperature regulation even in hot weather and extended the normal brewing season from seven months to ten or twelve months a year. The additional introduction of refrigerated ice cars on railroads in the 1870s "enabled beer to be sent long distances, irrespectively of the time of year, with the result that the export of the best South German breweries to other countries, as to France, has been greatly increased."[32]

Jacobsen then referenced the "recent important improvement" of ice machinery. The previous decade had seen several mild winters that prevented the collection of natural ice in enough quantity to satisfy the brewers and came at a great expense, inconvenience, and risk from Norway and the Alps. Ice machines went through many failed experiments before the von Linde system with ammonia came to be the most widely accepted. Other ice machines used the "compression of atmospheric air," distillation of ammonia, or the expansion of sulphurous acid but none were as successful or produced ice as cheaply as Carl von Linde's machines that made ice nearly as inexpensive as the purchase of natural ice.[33]

Between 1880 and 1884, Linde's machines came to be used in Germany, England, France, Italy, and Denmark. Between 1883 and 1884, over 100 Linde machines were sold to brewers. The Old Carlsberg brewery owned four itself, which collectively produced cold equivalent to the daily consumption of 200,000 lbs. of natural ice.[34] Jacobsen foresaw in 1884 that ice machines were soon to be indispensable for every brewery.

Jacobsen also noted that ice machines allowed for the regulation and control of fermentation all year and kept fermentation rooms clear of "smuts and mold spores, which natural ice contains," and enabled the surrounding air to be maintained in conditions of perfect purity. In addition, ice machines allowed for the "considerable geographic extension of the brewing industry" to warmer climates including the south of France, Italy, "and even hotter climates in other parts of the world." Even in 1884, Jacobsen foresaw the importance of refrigeration technology in the spread of lager brewing across the world.[35]

---

[32] Jacobsen, "Brewing Progress during the Last Fifty Years," 30.
[33] Jacobsen, "Brewing Progress during the Last Fifty Years," 30.
[34] Jacobsen, "Brewing Progress during the Last Fifty Years," 30.
[35] Jacobsen, "Brewing Progress during the Last Fifty Years," 30.

However, even with the need for regulated, controlled, dependable cold temperatures for fermentation and storage, most Continental brewers were initially hesitant to install artificial refrigeration systems into rooms containing vats of beer due to a fear of financial loss if the system failed. Yet, the shortage of space for ice storage forced large breweries like Spaten, Carlsberg in Denmark, and Heineken in Holland to try certain artificial refrigeration systems. The success of these breweries in the late 1870s and early 1880s in turn led to the spread of the system developed by Carl von Linde.[36]

Lager brewers were much quicker than British ale producers to adopt mechanized refrigeration. This was due to the colder temperature needs of lager brewing as well as the attitude that pervaded the German brewing industry that included a devotion to modern technological upgrades and the adoption of current scientific research about all aspects of the brewing process.

Responses to the spread of ice machines were not wholly positive, however. In 1876, the French brewing journal *Moniteur de la Brasserie* reported that German beer was becoming more popular in Great Britain and that establishments for lager were growing. In response, the British *Brewers' Journal* refuted their information, saying that:

> German beer will be drunk to a certain extent in London, as it is in Brussels, but to infer from this fact that it will invade the country is an illusion. England need not be alarmed. Its greatest enemy is the ice or artificial cold, which permits the fabrication of beer in its islands or in the Indies.[37]

This fear about the spread of artificial cold continued in the early 1880s as the *Brewers' Journal* noted the success of transporting meat from hot climates via ice machinery on a steamship and that as the machines come into more use, "it will have a considerable effect on brewing in hot climates."[38]

By the middle of the 1890s, the use of ice machines was widespread both in Britain and on the Continent. They were so prevalent among the large ale producers in England that they were likely to become used even among

---

[36] Richard W. Unger, *A History of Brewing in Holland, 900-1900 Economy, Technology, and the State* (Leiden; Boston: Brill, 2001), 365.

[37] "English vs. German Beer," *Brewers' Journal*, Vol. 11, 11/15/1876, 245.

[38] "Ice Machines," *Brewers' Journal*, Vol. 17, 4/15/1882, 110.

the small country brewers due to the enormous savings of liquor and time. Bringing together the "combined genius of modern engineering and modern chemistry" commentator Dr. W. Stanley Smith described the popular ammonia compression machines of von Linde's invention as "some of the most perfect types of machine the world has ever witnessed."[39]

Bottling Beer

Beer bottling also went through a revolution in the 1890s and early 1900s due to new techniques from lager breweries in the United States that built upon the Continental scientific knowledge and technology. By chilling, filtering, carbonating, and pasteurizing their beers, these breweries were able to sell beer that was always bottled fresh, star-bright, and without any sediment. In addition to the new bottling process, these American companies were able to mass-produce cheap glass bottles, bottle washers, and corking and labeling machines to further increase the efficiency and speed of bottling beer.[40]

Part II: Science in Brewing

Between the 1870s and the 1890s, a divide developed between what became known as scientific brewers and practical brewers. Practical brewers were the more traditional brewers who primarily had learned the basics of the brewing trade through experiential learning and apprenticeship instead of via formalized education about the biology, chemistry, and engineering that went into brewing beer. Scientific brewers were those who adopted the most up-to-date technology and incorporated the latest scientific knowledge of brewing processes into their own work. By the turn of the twentieth century, only scientific brewers were successful brewers, as breweries that did not make science a part of their work produced less consistent and less desirable beer for the consumers.

---

[39] "Modern Methods of Refrigeration," *Brewers' Journal*, Vol. 27, 10/15/1896, 642.
[40] Gourvish and Wilson, *The British Brewing Industry*, 299.

In Britain, a few forward-thinking breweries employed chemists fairly early on. Large brewers in Burton had employed chemists since 1845 when they were hired to combat the charges of adulteration of their beer from consumers. These were chemists of national distinction and who notably became head brewers themselves while working on learning more about the chemistry of barley, starches, and fermentable sugars including maltose.[41] Through the early 1880s, brewers in Burton were nearly the only ones to have brewing laboratories but, by the end of the decade, nearly every large British brewery had one, but they were very small with only one or two chemists who avoided collaboration with other brewing laboratories, severely limiting the broader accumulation of knowledge for the industry at large.[42]

The British brewing industry was unusual in its use of scientific procedures because although tertiary acceptance of scientific methods led to better products, brewers could produce beer that would sell without fully understanding the new scientific advances. In fact, many brewers overstressed their adherence to tradition and only grudgingly accepted scientific advances despite their skepticism.[43] However, for the most part this did not affect beer sales. The quality of the end product was more about taste than precision of process. Through reading brewing industry literature, modernizing brewing facilities and focusing more on cleanliness the British brewers produced beer the domestic markets thoroughly enjoyed.[44]

Though there had been some research regarding yeast and their life cycle in fermentation, the beginning of what becomes known as scientific brewing began with Louis Pasteur and his publication of *Études sur la Bière* (Studies on Beer) in 1876, with the English translation following in 1879.[45] Within this publication, Pasteur examined yeast, used in the fermentation of beer, and explained what yeast are and what they do in terms of beer production. He explains that yeast are single-celled living organisms and then goes on to

---

[41] Gourvish and Wilson, *The British Brewing Industry*, 59.

[42] C. C. Owen, *The Greatest Brewery in the World: A History of Bass, Ratcliff & Gretton* (Chesterfield: Derbyshire Record Society, 1992), 86; Gourvish and Wilson, *The British Brewing Industry*, 60.

[43] Gourvish and Wilson, *The British Brewing Industry*, 63.

[44] Gourvish and Wilson, *The British Brewing Industry*, 63.

[45] E. M. Sigsworth, "Science and the Brewing Industry, 1850–1900," *The Economic History Review*, New Series, Vol. 17 (3), 1965.

explain the life cycle of this organism in reference to beer and fermentation.[46] A basic synopsis is that the yeast ingests the fermentable sugars available in the wort—mostly from the malted grain but also from any additional sugars including honey, corn, cane sugar—and then converts the sugars into carbon dioxide and ethanol to transform the wort into beer.[47]

Understanding this process made it possible for brewers to then learn more about yeast and their life processes as well as to learn that there were many kinds of yeast, some that were better for certain beers than others as well as yeasts to avoid all together. However, control of the yeast and fermentation was still a few years away and needed the help of a botanist at the Carlsberg Brewery Laboratory in Copenhagen, Denmark.

Mashing Methods

Key to the brewing of quality beer is the amount of fermentable sugars that can be extracted from the malted grain during the mashing process. British and Continental brewers used two different methods for mashing, and while both produced enough liquor for the boil and sugars for the different kinds of fermentation, there were differing opinions about which produced better beer. The British, and most ale brewers, used an infusion mash while the Continental brewers, led by the Germans who had refined the technique, used a decoction method.

The infusion process is simpler and faster than decoction and continues to be a dominant method for mashing. The infusion method, as explained in Chapter 1, involves the steeping of the malted grains in hot water to extract the fermentable sugars for later fermentation. While today brewers use a standard temperature of around 150–5°F (65–8°C), British brewers of the eighteenth and nineteenth centuries tried several temperature levels to gain the most from their grains.

The second method of mashing, as developed and used by German and then other Continental brewers, is the decoction method. Decoction mashing

---

[46] Louis Pasteur, *Études Sur La Bière: Ses Maladies, Causes Qui Les Provoquent, Procédé Pour La Rendre Inaltérable; Avec Une Théorie Nouvelle De La Fermentation* (Paris: Gauthier-Villars, 1876).
[47] For a bit about why yeast does this, see Patrick E. McGovern, *Uncorking the Past: The Quest for Wine, Beer, and Other Alcoholic Beverages* (Berkeley: University of California Press, 2009), 2–6.

involves several more steps in an effort to extract as many fermentable sugars as possible from the grains. It was preferred to infusion by the Continental brewers because they believed that it made beer less intoxicating and more nutritious.[48] During decoction, a portion of the malt mash is boiled to gelatinize the starch from the gain completely and then added to the rest of the mash. This raises the temperature to the desired level of about 150°F (65°C). This method has some specific benefits compared with the infusion method preferred by the British even though it was more labor intensive. The most important benefit of decoction mashing is the higher yield of fermentable sugars. These are obtained because of the higher susceptibility of gelatinized starch to the amylases enzymes present in the malt. This leads to a more complete fermentation as well as a clearer beer due to the coagulation of part of the proteins during mashing which settle at the bottom of the fermentation vessel instead of remaining suspended in the beer and making it appear cloudy.[49]

The Keeping Qualities of Beer

The keeping qualities of beer are also very important in the commercial viability of any export trade, whether out of the region of a brewery or out of the country. There are few techniques to help with the keeping qualities of beer regardless of style or production methods, but over the nineteenth century brewers were able to develop different strategies to enhance the longevity of their products.

The British brewers depended upon two ingredients for keeping their ales palatable on a longer term for their consumers. The keeping qualities of higher alcohol content and an abundance of hops were well known.[50] For decades before the nineteenth century, the British brewing industry consistently depended upon these qualities in their beer for their products' longevity.[51]

---

[48] Jacobsen, "Brewing Progress during the Last Fifty Years," 30.
[49] Reedand Nagodawithana, *Yeast Technology* (New York: Van Nostrand Reinhold, 1991), 109.
[50] However, this knowledge did not actually lead to an intentional "invention" of the India Pale Ale as many have incorrectly supposed.
[51] Unger, *Beer in the Middle Ages and the Renaissance*, 55.

In spite of the positive influence of higher alcohol percentage for beer longevity, Continental lagers tended to have a long shelf life with a lower alcohol by volume (ABV) on average. This was due to the brewing and aging process. Due to the quick turnaround of British ales and the brewers' ambivalent interest in scientific precision, British beers were sold with a fair amount of sediment made up of living and dead yeast cells as well as small particles of hops, malt, and other organic matter left over from the brewing process. These organic particulates had the potential to be infected by airborne bacteria and wild yeasts if the barrels or bottles were not sealed correctly, or if they were left in direct sunlight which could cause what is known as "light strike"—a process that spoils beer.[52]

In comparison, Continental pilsners were aged for several months in cold temperatures, which allowed all sediment to settle to the bottom of the aging vessels. This allowed the brewers to bottle and cask the finished pilsner as a light-colored and clear lager beer that had little-to-no sediment. Not only was this aesthetically attractive,[53] but it also left little in the way of particulates that could be affected through further aging during travel and before sale. In spite of the lower ABV and fewer hops used, the lager was able to have a long shelf life that was equal to or longer than the British ales.[54]

In addition to the lagering process and the benefits of bottom fermentation, the higher carbonation of lager also helped its longevity. The gradual secondary fermentation at one to two degrees above freezing for several months produced lager beers that had a very high level of carbonation compared with British beers that were aged very quickly. Carbonation made the beer "refreshing" and acted as a preservative in its own right. With a high level of carbon dioxide in the beer there was less room for any free oxygen, and by eliminating most of the oxygen, the carbonation inhibited bacterial growth that would turn the beer sour, unpalatable, and unmarketable. This made it unnecessary for the beer to be as high in alcohol or brewed with as many hops as British ales were, leading to a crisper and less bitter flavor.[55] The lower ABV also had the added

---

[52] "Deposit in Bottled Beer," *Brewers' Journal*, Vol. 20, 4/15/1885, 141.
[53] See Chapter 5 for more on this.
[54] Nagodawithana, *Yeast Technology*, 93, 119.
[55] Jacobsen, "Brewing Progress during the Last Fifty Years," 30.

benefit of allowing consumers to have a greater quantity of beer without higher levels of inebriation which, in turn, supported higher production numbers to meet demands.

Pasteurization

In addition to his contribution to the knowledge of the microbial origin of fermentation and explanation of its anaerobic nature, Louis Pasteur also introduced a method for increasing the shelf life and stability of beer and other beverages.[56] Pasteur's technique, known as pasteurization, became popular both on the Continent and in the United States by the end of the 1870s and sterilizes the beer within its containers to avoid any microbial infections after fermentation. The first step was to carefully seal the beer "in bottles, corked with good sound cords, and securely fastened ... The bottles thus fastened should be placed up to the head in a trough of cold water." The water would then be gradually heated with a steam jacket or coil to about 145° to 160°F (63°–71°C) and kept there for an hour and a half. The water and the bottles would then gradually cool down to room temperature. Though, "some brewers affirm that for export it will be found advantageous to employ a higher degree of heat"[57] as the British *Country Brewers' Gazette* attested in 1879.

Modern brewers utilize pasteurization as well. Many use a tunnel pasteurizer through which bottled and canned beer passes through heating and cooling zones on a moving platform. The beer is heated to pasteurization temperature of approximately 140°F (60°C) over the course of about twenty minutes, kept there for ten minutes, and then cooled to 48°F (30°C) in approximately twenty more minutes. The total time it takes today for pasteurization is only about one hour, but the process and temperatures remain very similar to those of the second half of the nineteenth century.[58]

---

[56] Nagodawithana, *Yeast Technology*, 9.
[57] "The Pasteurisation of Beer," *The Country Brewers' Gazette*, Vol. 3, 4/16/1879, 155.
[58] Nagodawithana, *Yeast Technology*, 121.

Figure 2.3 Carlsberg Laboratory.

Pure Yeast

A particularly important scientific revolution in brewing occurred in Copenhagen in the early 1880s due to investigations into beer spoilage at the Carlsberg Brewery of J. C. Jacobsen. In 1871, Jacobsen established the Carlsberg Laboratory at the Carlsberg brewery in Copenhagen to study the science of malting, brewing, and fermentation. Emil Christian Hansen, a botanist, was hired in 1874 to head the laboratory's Physiological Department and to study the science of fermentation. The Carlsberg Laboratory set out to build on the work done by Louis Pasteur, who as we know had demonstrated that the yeast used for brewing were actually living single-celled organism responsible for the fermentation of sugars into alcohol and carbon dioxide.[59]

While bottom-fermented Bavarian-style beers had been produced at Carlsberg since 1846, there were still problems with the spoilage of beers. In 1882, Carlsberg began brewing beer all year round instead of only during the colder months between October and June. However, though it was now producing much more volume, large amounts of beer were becoming spoilt

---

[59] Nagodawithana, *Yeast Technology*, 8, 14.

for unknown reasons in spite of new refrigeration technology. Emil Christian Hansen, the head of the Physiology Department, was asked by J. C. Jacobsen to figure out a solution to the problem.[60]

Hansen's background in botany led him to go against the favored bacteriological-chemical approach of Pasteur who believed diseases in lager beers were from bacterial infection. Hansen adopted a botanical approach that identified the culprit in species of airborne and insect-born "wild yeasts." His work demonstrated that yeast cells could be infected, which would cause the beer to be spoilt, thus resulting in losses for the brewery. He also showed that there are many different types of yeast and that pure versions of these yeasts could be isolated and then propagated under controlled situations so that all yeast used in a beer's fermentation were exactly alike without any "wild" ones contaminating the process.[61]

In 1883, Hansen became the first person ever to isolate and propagate a single yeast cell using yeast from the Carlsberg brewery's strain, which he named *Saccharomyces Carlsbergensis* (though now known as *S. pastorianus*), after the brewery. Hansen's process transformed the brewing industry and is seen today as a landmark moment in the history of brewing and the science of fermentation.[62] Through the adoption of a "pure yeast" approach to beer fermentation, brewers are able to gain more precise consistency with their finished products. The ability to use the same yeast every time increased the control over the bottom-fermentation process adopted by much of Continental Europe by this time.[63]

Instead of keeping these findings secret for the brewery's own use, J. C. Jacobsen insisted that the results be published publicly in scientific journals and that descriptions of Hansen's process were shared with the brewing world. This way anyone could build equipment for the isolation and

---

[60] Teich, "The Industrialization of Brewing in Germany (1800–1914)," in *Production, Marketing, and Consumption of Alcoholic Beverages since the Late Middle Ages*, 112.
[61] Gourvish and Wilson, *The British Brewing Industry*, 59.
[62] Nagodawithana, *Yeast Technology*, 112.
[63] Teich, "The Industrialization of Brewing in Germany (1800–1914)," in *Production, Marketing, and Consumption of Alcoholic Beverages since the Late Middle Ages*, 112.

propagation of their own brewery's yeast strains and use Hansen's methods. In addition, samples of the Carlsberg yeast were sent upon request to breweries around the world, including Heineken in Amsterdam—now one of the top two beer producers in the world in 2021—and brewers were even allowed to visit at Carlsberg to learn the new methods, a much different approach than the isolated secrecy of British breweries.[64]

While many brewers on the Continent took this new information and used it for their own brewing purposes, most British brewers were not as keen on utilizing this scientific approach to brewing. British brewers, in the face of the productivity and quality of scientific brewers on the Continent, still considered their older, traditional methods to be the way to produce the best beer.[65] However, at least one English journalist noted that "it would be impossible to produce in England a stable beer [like those of Bavaria] without adopting scientific means for determining stability."[66]

Conclusion

As Sigsworth notes, the Pasteurian revolution in beer brewing had little effect on brewing practices in Britain.[67] "In no case can scientific discovery be said to have had revolutionary effects upon the brewing industry."[68] While Continental lager brewers adopted the latest in technological and scientific innovations to produce a beer style that appealed to consumers the world over, British breweries continued to hold onto their traditional practices and styles.

Through the use of steam engines, mechanized refrigeration, and scientific knowledge about yeast and pasteurization, the Continental brewers were able

---

[64] Keith Gribbins, "The 40 Biggest Breweries in the World in 2021," *Craft Brewing Business*, June 13, 2022, https://www.craftbrewingbusiness.com/business-marketing/the-40-biggest-breweries-in-the-world-in-2021/, accessed October 7, 2022.

[65] T. G. Parsons, "Science and the Victorian Brewing Industry, 1870–1900" in *Production, Marketing, and Consumption of Alcoholic Beverages since the Late Middle Ages: Session B-14: Proceedings, Tenth International Economic History Congress, Leuven, August 1990*, eds. International Economic History Congress, Aerts Erik Cullen L. M. Wilson R. G. (Leuven, Belgium, 1990), 114.

[66] "Consumption of Beer," *Brewers' Journal*, 9/15/1890, 562.

[67] Sigsworth, "Science and the Brewing Industry, 1850–1900," 541.

[68] T. G. Parsons, "Science and the Victorian Brewing Industry, 1870–1900" in "Production, Marketing, and Consumption of Alcoholic Beverages since the Late Middle Ages," 114.

to produce a consistent and palatable product. Their lager beers were able to keep for long periods of time and over great distances without their producers worrying about spoilage or their consumers worrying about what the finished product would taste like, or look like, when it arrived in their hands.

The best beer of the nineteenth century, and up the present, is a consistent beer. Consistency is king. Consumers, once they find a product they like, do not want it to change, they want to receive what they expect. In the pilsner beers produced by Continental brewers, they found a beer that they could depend upon and trust through the use of scientific processes and the adoption of the latest technology. By consciously ignoring the technological, Pasteurian, and Pure Yeast revolutions in brewing the British brewing industry fell far behind the Continental brewers when it came to gaining new consumers as the nineteenth century moved toward its end.

3

Making the Investments Count: Business Strategies of Brewing Industries

Introduction

By the end of the nineteenth century the golden pilsner lager beer produced by German and other Continental brewing industries had overtaken ales produced by the British in just about every beer market in the world outside the British Isles. An important part of the explanation for why this occurred was Continental brewers' adoption of new business strategies to raise investment capital and gain new markets for their products. In addition, the insistence of Continental brewers on educating their employees in the latest science and technology helped them succeed in relation to British brewers.

Greater investment capital meant that Continental lager breweries were able to expand and upgrade their brewing facilities to be more competitive. expansion meant that the Continental brewers could capitalize on economies of scale and sell their products more cheaply than their competitors. Economies of scale meant that the greater the volume of beer produced, the lower the cost of each beer. Thus, large breweries had a significant cost advantage over smaller ones.[1] It was expensive to invest in newer technologies and machines, but the increases, and possible changes, in production were well worth the costs. Lager beer prices dropped toward the end of the nineteenth century because economies of scale helped increase demand. Alcoholic beverages, including beer, tend to have a high rate of substitution and are particularly responsive to changes in price. This means that less

---

[1] Alfred Chandler and Takashi Hikino, *Scale and Scope: The Dynamics of Industrial Capitalism* (Cambridge, MA: Belknap Press, 1990), 23.

expensive alcoholic beverages will sell in greater quantities regardless of consumers' personal drink preferences. Thus, I argue here that producers of lager benefited greatly from utilizing changes in technology and management that resulted in greater economies of scale.[2]

From the 1870s through the early 1890s many technical and business innovations helped propel Continental lagers outward from their production centers to the detriment of the British brewing industry. While British brewers were producing more product than ever before and Guinness and Bass were the largest and most productive breweries in the world, respectively, their influence and impact on the markets outside of home consumption declined considerably. The reasons for this were that their market strategies and goals remained focused on retaining local markets without realizing or attempting to control the vast foreign markets available to them via the imperial territories and trade networks of the British Empire. The brewing industry remained highly traditional in production and very conservative in its business leadership.[3]

There have been two key studies looking at the industrialization of Germany vis-à-vis Great Britain, but these have focused on industries other than brewing. Alfred Chandler and Takashi Hikino's *Scale and Scope* examines the evolution of modern industrial enterprise in a comparative approach that looks at the United States, Germany, and Great Britain. They argue that the decline of Britain as an industrial force, when compared with the other two nations, was because of its failure to make a three-pronged investment in production, distribution, and management to exploit economies of scale and scope within the window of opportunity available to them at the end of the nineteenth century.[4] While they briefly touch upon the brewing industries in Britain and Germany, they focus more on branded, packaged products, electrical equipment, and other industries. In addition, Johann Peter Murmann's *Knowledge and Competitive Advantage* builds upon Chandler and Hikino's work with an examination of

---

[2] John J. McCusker, "Distilling and Its Implications for the Atlantic World of the 17th and 18th Centuries," in *Production, Marketing, and Consumption of Alcoholic Beverages since the Late Middle Ages: Proceedings of the Tenth International Economic History Cong (Studies in Social and Economic History)*, eds. Erik Aerts, L. Cullen, and R. Wilson (Ithaca, NY: Cornell University Press, 1990), 7–8.

[3] Gourvish and Wilson, *Production, Marketing, and Consumption*, 122.

[4] Chandler and Hikino, *Scale and Scope*, 286.

the synthetic dye industry in Germany, the United States, and Great Britain. Murmann's work argues for a dynamic model of competitive advantage wherein successful synthetic dye firms all had close connections with national institutions, including universities and the government. Successful companies were able to cooperate through collective action to mold the social and institutional environment in which they operated, and German firms like Bayer were the best at this.[5] This chapter builds upon these approaches to the history of industry in order to explain the relative decline of the British brewing industry and the loss in popularity of its beer styles in comparison to the spread of pilsner as the Continental brewing firms surpassed the British.

This chapter begins with the different approaches to business structures and investment by Continental and British breweries. While Continental lager breweries utilized a managerial hierarchical approach, British breweries were usually personally managed by founders or their families. These two approaches were not equal in raising capital or in defining the long-term goals of the brewing firms. Continental approaches led to better exploitation of economies of scale and in capturing overseas markets.

The following section deals with differing approaches to export markets. While the lager brewers of the Continent sought out and gained control of foreign markets, the British almost completely ignored overseas markets in order to concentrate on national market control. By neglecting foreign markets between 1880 and 1900, British brewers lost the opportunity to capitalize on the colonial markets of the British Empire as well as other potentially lucrative overseas profits.

The third and final section of the chapter examines the different educational approaches of Continental and British brewers. The brewing industries in Continental Europe responded quickly to the needs of lager breweries by establishing professional programs for training brewers and managers. These programs included detailed instruction in the latest science and technology as well as management strategies. These managers studied the latest strategies for marketing, production organization, and distribution. In comparison, British breweries relied upon familial connections and social connections in choosing

---

[5] Johann Peter Murmann, *Knowledge and Competitive Advantage: The Coevolution of Firms, Technology, and National Institutions* (New York: Cambridge University Press, 2003), Preface, 3–5.

managers for their firms. Without formal institutionalized brewing education available, brewers and managers learned on the job via apprenticeships or via clerking in finance departments. The lack of formal education meant that British brewers did not have the same opportunities as Continental brewers to learn how science and new technological innovations could benefit beer production and distribution.

During the last thirty years of the nineteenth century Continental lager beer production outperformed British brewing companies on a global scale. The reasons for this are that they formed Joint-Stock Companies and Limited Liability Companies before (and with greater success than) British brewing firms, they intentionally focused on their export trade as an area of growth, and they recognized the importance of professional education and employee training. These choices in investment and business strategy helped the pilsner gain control over foreign beer markets.

Formation of LLCs and Joint-Stock Companies

Continental Brewing Industry

Most breweries in Europe before the 1880s were privately held companies and were usually run by families or small partnerships. Ownership and management tended to be hereditary regardless of the size of the brewery. However, beginning in the 1860s and 1870s, the incorporation of brewing firms gained traction and spread quickly in Germany and elsewhere on the Continent. The popularity and benefits of incorporation as Limited Liability Companies (LLCs), also known as Joint-Stock Companies or *Aktienbrauerei*, only began in the UK after Guinness went public in 1886. UK brewers met with varying degrees of success. Some brewing firms (including Guinness) succeeded very well, while others floundered under poor management. German LLCs, however, were able to turn their investment capital into up-to-date breweries with the latest technology to produce high-quality lagers in large quantities. Investment strategies through incorporation are an important mechanism by which the pilsner-style was able to spread so far around the world and why the influence of British brewing declined.

The popularity of LLCs for the German brewing industry began very quickly in the late 1860s across the soon-to-be unified German Empire. In 1870, private individuals owned all of the breweries in the Bavarian capital of Munich until several banking houses in the city formed the First Munich Joint-Stock Company in order to "carry on business on an enlarged scale."[6] The bankers had incorporated and purchased the Zenker Brewery with all of its equipment, cellars, stock, and materials and opened the company shares for purchase around the region for public investment. Due to the good condition of the brewery and its close proximity to a railway station, the shareholders expected to receive a dividend from their shares during that first year. The railroad access would give the new company "great advantage, as it will enable the Company to send their produce at a very trifling charge to any part of the kingdom, or, indeed, of the Continent."[7] Not only did this early incorporation foreshadow a movement toward LLCs but it also shows the early intentions of the new owners to export their products using new funds and by exploiting economies of scale.

The costs of lager production demanded large amounts of investment capital due to the needs of the brewing process. While British beer had a relatively quick turnaround of a few weeks, as we saw in Chapters 1 and 2, lager brewers had to deal with an extended production time that required lagering in ice caves for several months. The need for extensive temperature control as well as the time commitment meant that brewing companies had to wait for a return on their investment. However, there were plenty of investors who saw the profit potential for lager breweries, and Munich was soon not alone in having an *Aktienbrauerei*.

Munich was not the only city where joint-stock companies were starting to form. The *Brewers' Journal* reported that in 1870 Berlin there were forty-eight breweries, all owned and worked by private brewers, except for the recently incorporated Tivoli Brewery. In addition, eighteen of these breweries were brewing only "Bavarian Beer" (one of the names for the bottom-fermented golden lagers), while nineteen made *Weißbier*, with 50 percent wheat, and nine brewed brown beer, showing the growing popularity of the pilsner-style.[8] Another joint-stock company received a concession by the Prussian Minister for Commerce and Public Works in Frankfort-on-the-Oder, known as the

---

[6] "Joint-Stock Company at Munich," *Brewers' Journal*, 1/15/1870, 6.
[7] "Joint-Stock Company at Munich," 6.
[8] "Berlin Breweries," *Brewers' Journal*, 1/15/1870, 7.

"Frankforter Actian-Brauerei" within the year.[9] In 1871, three more joint-stock breweries formed in Bavaria with an emphasis on exportation of "Bavarian beer" and the need for incorporation because "its' manufacture requires the use of enormous capital"[10] as well as three more in Berlin, following Tivoli's lead, and one in Saxony.[11] The popularity of incorporation continued through 1871 in Germany. During the first six months "the rage for transforming private breweries of old standing into joint-stock companies" persisted with eleven new companies in Berlin. All their shares were bought up immediately, with many of them "already commanding considerable premium" within months.[12]

The movement to incorporate continued through the 1870s, though it had both advocates and opponents. The trend to concentrate capital in large establishments led many small breweries to close up shop because of increased competition. While the concentration of capital and the "co-operative principle" were beneficial because they lowered the cost of production, there were opponents who denounced the "monopolist" brewers and the movement to put the brewing trade into the "hands of a few large capitalists, who order things pretty much as they like."[13] While there was similar talk in England regarding the power of the larger brewers, it was "much more conspicuous in Germany," according to the British *Brewers' Journal*. The benefits of incorporation, however, were in the numbers. While the number of breweries in Germany had declined by 10 percent, the production average of each brewery was 50 percent greater in 1877 than in 1873.[14]

The *Moniteur de la Brasseries*, a French brewers' journal, responded to this information with its own statistics in 1878, showing that the number of breweries continually declined, while production increased every year. The author argued that "from this fact the inference is drawn that the breweries of the future are the large breweries" because the fact that small breweries cannot successfully compete with the large ones is "undeniable."[15] The future proved

---

[9] "New Brewery Companies in Germany," *Brewers' Journal*, 9/15/1870, 188.
[10] "Brewing in Bavaria," *Brewers' Journal*, 9/15/1870, 189.
[11] "Brew Brewery Companies in Germany," *Brewers' Journal*, 9/15/1871, 210.
[12] "New Brewery Companies in Germany," *Brewers' Journal*, 9/15/1871, 223.
[13] "Large v. Small Breweries," *Brewers' Journal*, 6/15/1877, 151.
[14] "Large v. Small Breweries," *Brewers' Journal*, 3/15/1878, 151.
[15] "Large v. Small Breweries," 69.

this sentiment correct. By 1911, less than 10 percent of German breweries produced 37 percent of all the beer in the country.[16]

Exploiting economies of scale was not the only way Continental breweries excelled. The cooperation between breweries had several benefits outside of the scientific and technological advances discussed in the previous chapter. Large brewing firms, like other large managerial firms in Germany, preferred to cooperate for market share and profit and shared a belief in industrial cooperation, unlike those in Britain.[17] This cooperation did for the brewing industry the same that it did for the synthetic dye industry: it made the industry a united force that led to better institutional benefits from the government through effective lobbying.[18] This did not go unnoticed by British brewers, who observed that the German Brewers' Association was able to act "with authority as the representative of the interests of the trade" in comparison to a recent failed attempt to begin a British brewers club in 1876.[19] The British did not cooperate due to the long-standing traditions of secrecy in the industry. Unlike the German brewers who saw industrial cooperation as a benefit, British brewers only saw each other as competition due to the importance of regional markets. By seeking out export markets, the Germans avoided the national competition that hindered British cooperation.

J. C. Jacobsen, founder of the Carlsberg Brewery in Copenhagen, echoed these sentiments in 1884, in his retrospective address about the previous fifty years of brewing. Small breweries were indeed less numerous in the present, he conceded, and whereas fifty years earlier it was rare to find breweries producing 10,000 hectoliters annually, by 1884 there were several breweries producing as much as 100,000 to 500,000 hectoliters a year. He argued that small breweries were unable to compete with larger companies because they could not cover the higher taxation of beer in recent years, or indeed the rising prices of raw materials that came with increased competition.[20]

---

[16] Chandler and Hikino, *Scale and Scope*, 433.
[17] Chandler and Hikino, *Scale and Scope*, 395.
[18] Murmann, *Knowledge and Competitive Advantage*, 181. In regards to the success of the German Association for Patent Protection in getting patent law on a legislative agenda.
[19] "The German Brewers," *Brewers' Journal*, 6/15/1876, 136.
[20] J. C. Jacobsen, "Brewing Progress during the Last Fifty Years," *Brewers' Journal*, 1/15/1885, 110.

Figure 3.1 J. C. Jacobsen, Carlsberg Brewery, 1886.

Jacobsen went on to point out the many benefits of large, mostly urban, breweries, including facilities to send beer "by railroad, in perfect condition, in ice-cars." The transition from a large brewery to a huge manufacturer, like Carlsberg, offered numerous and important improvements that made beer production more cost-effective through economies of scale. These included the opportunity to gain "superior knowledge, and so excel their fellows in intelligence and skill" as well as afford all of the latest scientific apparatus in order to utilize the latest scientific advances.[21]

In spite of these sentiments, Jacobsen warned that the trend of incorporation into joint-stock companies was "a disadvantageous change, and one fraught with peril to the future of the brewing industry" even though privately held "breweries with a capital reckoned in millions" would likely be bought up or incorporated.[22] Jacobsen's opposition came from his years as founder and owner of one of the largest and most forward-thinking breweries in Europe. His worries stemmed from the possible influence of shareholders who sought only large dividends to the detriment of improving the brewery. As he argued in 1884:

> Many brewing companies have thus gone down, some so low that it will be difficult, if not impossible, for them to recover themselves. Bitter experience, learned in so many quarters, of the evils of this one-sided economy should open the eyes of shareholders, and as speculative swindles and the fantastic dreams, which see a gold mine in every brewery, vanish from the scene, a new race of shareholders, who have bought their shares at something like their real value, may be expected to prove more rational.[23]

However, most of the brewing companies on the Continent and elsewhere ignored Jacobsen's warnings. Within just two years of his address, the first UK brewery went public and started the trend among British breweries as well. Yet the economic benefits of incorporation on the Continent had already pushed its lager breweries ahead of those in the UK. Not only were the lager breweries able to consistently update their production facilities with the funds gained by going public, their focus on the exportation of their product, unlike UK breweries, ensured that regional beer markets did not become oversaturated.

---

[21] Jacobsen, "Brewing Progress," 110.
[22] Jacobsen, "Brewing Progress," 110.
[23] Jacobsen, "Brewing Progress," 110.

Figure 3.2 Spaten Brewery, Late Nineteenth Century.

The Brewing Industry in the UK

The brewers in the UK were much slower in their adoption of incorporation and once they began, they had mixed results. Some brewing companies excelled while others became examples of what not to do. The UK brewing firms had already developed their own strategies of business organization over the previous century through close partnerships before the popularity and benefits of incorporation and outside investment became too tantalizing to ignore.

Concentration of the brewing industry in the UK was evident by the 1880s with about 2,000 breweries centered in and around London, Dublin, and Edinburgh as well as growing development in Burton, Tadcaster, Alton, Wrexham, and Newark. However, the boom years for the industry between 1860 and 1880 were coming to an end as consumption declined and the temperance movement gained strength.[24] Over the course of the 1880s, larger breweries in the UK acquired many of their smaller commercial competitors and focused on the purchase of pubs, beer-houses, and off-licenses. These strategies built up their tied trade, assuring themselves markets for selling their products by owning and controlling the locations which sold beer.[25] However, in the middle of the 1880s an important change occurred that disrupted the brewing industry's previous business strategy.

On October 25, 1886, Guinness incorporated into a public LLC and raised £6 million immediately. This was a big surprise for the rest of the UK brewing industry and set off a rush of breweries to incorporate. The incorporation of Guinness transformed the structure and policies of the brewing industry in the UK but did not affect brewery management.[26]

Prior to Guinness going public, UK brewers had used other strategies to promote and expand their businesses. The most popular way to do this was through partnerships, many of which had begun around the turn of the nineteenth century. A large British brewery would have eight to ten partners running the company who were usually family members or men with whom the founder had close social ties. The partners would all be shareholders in the brewing firm and control the profits and business strategies.[27] Most large brewers, including those in London, focused on generating capital internally through these partnerships. Family connections and savings banks were the primary places for procuring loans.[28] Partners in large breweries were both rich and influential and were usually among the only people who could see the

---

[24] T. R. Gourvish and R. G. Wilson, *The British Brewing Industry, 1830–1980* (New York: Cambridge University Press, 1994), 126.

[25] Gourvish and Wilson, *The British Brewing Industry*, 126.

[26] Gourvish and Wilson, *The British Brewing Industry*, 250.

[27] Gourvish and Wilson, *The British Brewing Industry*, 86.

[28] Gourvish and Wilson, *The British Brewing Industry*, 229, 232.

brewery's accounts and brewing books, limiting the possibility of innovation in the process.[29] Without collaboration and discussion about brewing methods, breweries and brewery workers would continue to use the same processes and methods as those before them had used, regardless of whether they were the most efficient ways to brew or not. Without new perspectives or input, British breweries stagnated in their secrecy. Most breweries were entrepreneurial at the start and founders, as well as their heirs, retained control of management through the nineteenth century. They viewed their businesses in personal instead of organizational terms, "as family estates to be nurtured and passed on to heirs."[30] Though partners usually had a basic education in how to brew beer, they usually focused on finance and business.[31] While the brewing companies of the Continent focused on expansion, the sharing of technology, and scientific innovation through organized brewing schools like those at the Carlsberg Laboratory, the British remained secretive and closed to outside influence as they continued to educate via apprenticeship programs alone.[32] The British devotion to personal management slowed the development of the functional and administrative skills necessary to maintain a market share and to grow by exploiting competitive capabilities. In addition, British brewers moved overseas hesitantly and less successfully than foreign competitors.[33]

This approach to management by the British is known as personal capitalism, and brewing firms were not the only ones to follow this strategy.[34] As in other industries, British breweries tended to be closely managed by the founders and heirs. Even after they were incorporated and managerial hierarchies were recruited, the founding family or families continued to be influential stockholders and senior executives in their own companies. They would directly supervise middle and often lower-level managers and, as

---

[29] Gourvish and Wilson, *The British Brewing Industry*, 234.
[30] Chandler and Hikino, *Scale and Scope*, 286.
[31] Gourvish and Wilson, *The British Brewing Industry*, 244. See pages 20–1 below as well.
[32] Mikuláš Teich, *Bier, Wissenschaft und Wirtschaft in Deutschland 1800–1914: ein Beitrag zur deutschen Industrialisierungsgeschichte* (Wien: Böhlau, 2000), 104–5. Translation by Malcolm F. Purinton with support from Google Translate. And Gourvish and Wilson, *The British Brewing Industry*, 61–63.1
[33] Chandler and Hikino, *Scale and Scope*, 294.
[34] Chandler and Hikino, *Scale and Scope*, Chapter 7.

mentioned earlier, promotions were usually due to personal ties and social position instead of merit.[35] This led to few salaried managers running British breweries in comparison to German brewing companies. Legacy managers took business decisions personally instead of looking toward future investments in expansion and distribution. In general, British industrialists seemed to have a distrust of losing personal control over enterprises they had either created or inherited.[36] Because managers came through hereditary successions within the firms, instead of promotion through merit, ensuring long-term continuity of the company's direction was uncertain.[37] Having a capacity for business that could turn a profit or loyalty to the firm was not hereditary. For example, after the heir to the Truman Brewery in London died in 1885, the family decided to withdraw and liquidate their shares, which led to the incorporation of the brewery in the late 1880s.[38] By not turning to trained managers, the British brewers failed to realize the potential of economies of scale through investing in production, distribution, and management.[39] Even with the move toward incorporation, the former partners and families were intent on retaining their control of the future of the breweries.

Without investment in manufacturing, marketing, and management, the British brewing firms were unable to exploit the economies of scale as well as the Continental brewers.[40] The British did have continuing opportunities for profit with a rich domestic consumer market, but this led to fewer investments in growth outside of the region and a loss of overseas markets.[41] Continental brewers who invested in research and management of their firms were able to succeed where the British failed.[42] Due to their success in exploiting economies of scale, the Continental brewers needed new markets to continue to make profits for their shareholders and it is to export strategies that we now turn.

---

[35] Chandler and Hikino, *Scale and Scope*, 240, 242.
[36] Chandler and Hikino, *Scale and Scope*, 286.
[37] Gourvish and Wilson, *The British Brewing Industry*, 235.
[38] Gourvish and Wilson, *The British Brewing Industry*, 86.
[39] Chandler and Hikino, *Scale and Scope*, 286.
[40] Chandler and Hikino, *Scale and Scope*, 393.
[41] Chandler and Hikino, *Scale and Scope*, 284–5, 291.
[42] Chandler and Hikino, *Scale and Scope*, 433–4.

Exports

Investment strategies were not the only differences between brewers on the Continent and those in the UK. They also differed in their geographic foci for their products. The domestic markets for Continental breweries—including Denmark, Germany, and Austria—were strong and consumption per head was among the highest in the world. Similarly, the domestic markets in Britain were also lucrative, with the brewing firms spending most of their time and money competing for control. The most important difference was that while the British and Irish brewers focused almost exclusively on domestic beer consumption and competition between each other, the Germans and other Continental brewers used their resources to target export markets in Europe, the European colonies, and other foreign markets from South America to Asia.

The difference in priority given to export markets had substantial, though very different, consequences for ale and lager breweries. By the end of the nineteenth century, the British, who nearly had a monopoly over beer exported to ports around the world up to 1880,[43] had lost strength in foreign beer markets, including those of their own colonies.[44] The influence of the Continental brewing industries, however, promoted both the consumption of pilsner beers in export markets as well as the production of lagers by European settlers. The spread of German beers, in particular, was an object of pride for the Germen brewing journals. For instance, the *Allegemeine Brauer&Hopfen-Zeitung* went to great lengths to report the presence of German lagers in foreign ports including African ports, Hong Kong, Argentina, and British India throughout the 1880s and 1890s.[45]

---

[43] Gourvish and Wilson, *The British Brewing Industry*, 173–5.
[44] As examined in Chapter 4 with South Africa.
[45] "Einfuhr deutsher Biere in Hongkong," *Allegemeine Brauer&Hopfen-Zeitung*, 6/15/1882, 399; "Deutsches Bier in Afrika," *Allegemeine Brauer&Hopfen-Zeitung*, 7/30/1882, 526; "Bierbrauerei in Japan," *Allegemeine Brauer&Hopfen-Zeitung*, 2/16/1887, 223; "Bierexport nach Argentinien," *Allegemeine Brauer&Hopfen-Zeitung*, 3/27/1887, 427; "Deutsches Bier in Britisch-Indien," *Allegemeine Brauer&Hopfen-Zeitung*, 2/2/1890, 202.

German and Continental Beer Exportation

The entrepreneurial motivations of German brewers, and those who liked their beer, led to more than the incorporation of breweries to gain investment capital for expansion and technological advancement. New brewery LLCs were motivated to seek new markets outside their regional or local locations due to high levels of competition with other German breweries, which pushed them to increase production while maintaining quality through the latest science and technology.

An example from 1869 in Germany shows an early awareness of the potential for foreign markets. In 1869, beer purchased from the newly incorporated Tivoli brewery in Berlin arrived in Hakodadi, Japan for the German consul of the North German Confederation, who sold it locally, including to the Japanese Governor of the Island of Jesso. In spite of an eight-month voyage, the beer arrived in excellent condition and the Governor stated his preference for the lager beer of Tivoli over all others. Even more importantly, he wanted to buy more. In response, the Tivoli Brewery Company received several fresh orders for large quantities of their lager that shipped from Hamburg in 1870 and helped the brewery establish itself in Japan.[46] Instead of viewing the Japanese market as too far away or of minimal importance, Tivoli increased their production to meet demand that led to greater foreign sales as well as better returns for European investors in the brewery. The British reported in the same year that 2,000,000 gallons of beer were sent to China and Japan from England and Germany. While English porter, ale, and stout were most popular, the Bavarian style was a close second. British brewers feared that the Continental lagers would, as one brewer wrote, "form a serious rival to the English beer in the Far East … We are so accustomed to grandiloquent reports from Germany about the beer trade, that we make always a considerable mental reservation in such cases." The same article went on to argue that it "may be worth our brewers' while to try lighter beers for certain warm countries than they at present export … [with] less strength and cheapness."[47] The inference here is that the popularity of pilsner had spread from Continental Europe to

---

[46] "Berlin Beer in Japan," *Brewers' Journal*, 3/15/1870, 48.
[47] "Beer in China and Japan," *Brewers' Journal*, 5/15/1870, 108.

the markets of East Asia and British brewers would have to develop new beer styles in order to compete internationally.

Although Germany exported a lot of beer, it still imported some from the UK. While there was an increase in imports into the port of Bremen, Germany in 1873, they were "eclipsed by the magnitude and importance of the export trade." The quality of beer coming out of Bremen was notable in the increased competitiveness with British exports in "South America and other transatlantic and distant places." The breweries that produced the lagers for export in 1872 "produced more than double what they brewed only five years ago," with their principle markets in New York and other US ports.[48] Production for export was a major motivation for the brewers in Bremen as well as those who shipped their own beer, from Bavaria for instance, to the port or for further export. In 1879, for instance, Bavaria exported a considerable 868,103 hectoliters, much of it to northern Germany. This was because northern German breweries were unable to keep up with domestic demand themselves having consumed 20,840,129 hectoliters in 1877–8.[49]

Exportation grew so quickly that it became a point of frustration within Germany. The British Consul of the Grand Duchy of Baden reported that the years 1895–9 were very successful years for brewers there. However, "the rage in Germany for exportation prevails to such an extent that every town exports its beer to other towns."[50] This led to interregional competition between breweries, prompting many to seek out foreign markets instead. This was in stark contrast to British brewers who sought to only control local and regional beer markets via the tied trade without turning their gazes overseas.

However, 1898 was the beginning of a severe decline in exports from northern German ports. In Hamburg, which had fifteen large breweries that produced over 22 million gallons of beer a year—with the ability to increase that by another 9 million a year—there was a noted decline in pasteurized export beers.[51] The decline of the export trade was unforeseen and due to a remarkable development in worldwide lager production between 1880 and 1890. Due to the popularity of the pilsner in overseas ports, the export trade now had

---

[48] "Beer Trade at Bremen in 1872," *Brewers' Journal*, 5/15/1873, 127.
[49] "German Beer Statistics," *Country Brewers' Gazette*, 2/5/1879, 55.
[50] "Free Trade in Beer and Its Results," *Brewers' Journal*, 6/15/1899, 321.
[51] "The Production and Export of Beer at Hamburg," *Brewers' Journal*, 12/15/1898, 891–2.

competition with locally built lager breweries in the countries of their overseas markets. This was especially noticeable in the best markets for German beer including the United States, British India, Australia, and South Africa.[52]

UK Beer Exports

While most of the wealth generated in Great Britain over the course of the nineteenth century came from the export performance of most of its key industries, the brewing industry was an outlier. Textiles, engineering, shipbuilding, and coal all thrived via export-oriented growth, while no more than 3 percent of the total output of the British brewing industry went for export.[53] Prior to 1911–13 the peak of British beer exportation was in 1859, with only 614,000 barrels exported out of over 15 million barrels of beer produced by England and Wales.[54] This was in spite of the fact that beer consumption and trade were part of British exploration and colonialism. As the British economic historians T. R. Gourvish and R. Wilson argued: "Wherever British settlers colonized land, in the East and West Indies, in America, in Ireland, and eventually Australasia, a demand for the native drink of their homeland was established." However, due to the warmer colonial climates, lack of good raw materials and technology (including mechanized refrigeration), it was impossible to produce even tolerable imitations of favorite British beer styles.[55]

In addition, shipping was very difficult. Beer is bulky and unstable, the price of exported beer was high, and brewers had to wait a long time for payment. Only a small number of brewers and bottling firms in the UK had the expertise, commitment, and capital needed to export beer. These included the Burton brewers Bass and Allsopp, some Scottish brewers in Edinburgh and Alloa, Guinness, and some bottlers in London and Liverpool.[56] Bass, the largest ale brewery in the world, exported a quarter of its production in the

---

[52] "The Production and Export of Beer at Hamburg," 891–2.
[53] Gourvish and Wilson, *British Brewing Industry*, 169. In comparison, German exports in 1885 were 5 percent of total production. However, the three largest export breweries at Bremen were not included in this percentage. The fact that Germany had breweries built only for export markets shows the importance to the industry. "Beer in Germany, 1880–1890," *Brewers' Journal*, 6/15/1891, 314–15.
[54] Gourvish and Wilson, *The British Brewing Industry*, 172, 600.
[55] Gourvish and Wilson, *The British Brewing Industry*, 169.
[56] Gourvish and Wilson, *The British Brewing Industry*, 169, 171.

1840s. In 1882, the *Brewers' Journal* noted that bottled Bass ale was "found in every country where Englishmen had yet put foot."[57] However, Bass exports dropped to only 10 percent in the early 1890s with domestic trade through tied houses and the agency system of off-license and distribution continuing to take precedence.[58] While the major beer producers concentrated on their domestic markets, it did not mean that there were no concerns over the loss of foreign markets. Trade journals attempted to take the major brewers to task for their low export numbers.

In fact, fear of German competition abroad was a recurring theme in the British brewing industry's journals between 1870 and 1900. While there had been increasing exports of ale and beer for three decades before 1870, by 1874 the *Brewers' Journal* reported increased competition from other countries. Some "over-wise gentlemen" were predicting that the Germans would soon beat the British out of foreign markets due to Germans manufacturing "at a cheaper rate a better article," which they sold "at terms with which the English brewer cannot compete." The reasons for this, they argued, included the adoption of science, which the English "of course neglect, and is generally to be looked forward to as the beer supplier of the future." While these arguments were proven correct within fifteen years, at this time the English commentator concluded, "such arguments are wholly false and unfounded. Our beer trade is shown to be increasingly largely [sic], and will increase largely, notwithstanding the well-intentioned efforts of our Teutonic friends."[59] In an article in 1876, another columnist attempted to assuage fears of German encroachment into British beer markets. The author agreed with a correspondent that German brewers had made great strides in their production. But, he was amused to think that there was any threat to the British "national beverage," saying "there is nothing to fear for the safety of English beer [because] it continues to be drunk in ever increasing quantities."[60] He then noted that "we will say nothing" about the export of British beer or "its consumption in foreign countries," inferring that readers already knew the trade was excellent.[61]

[57] Gourvish and Wilson, *The British Brewing Industry*, 75.
[58] Gourvish and Wilson, *The British Brewing Industry*, 92–4, 171.
[59] "Trade progress," *Brewers' Journal*, 4/15/1874, 75.
[60] "Trop de Zele," *Brewers' Journal*, 10/15/1876, 224.
[61] "Trop de Zele," 224.

Commentators and writers for the British brewing industry journals continued to support belief in UK brewing dominance. Reports often exclaimed that English beer was in universal demand, with exports doing so well that "it may be remarked of [English] beer—it has simply conquered the world." Evidence of the universal popularity of British beer over other national brewing industries was in "the extensive exports of the article to all parts of the habitable globe."[62] Though it is true that British beer reached ports all over the world, the amounts themselves, as explained above, were negligible and the writers' arguments lacked any supporting statistics to hold up their claims.

As news of lager beer, its popularity, and its expansion reached the UK regularly, some British brewers even tried their hand at making their own lagers. However, this was a controversial and largely unsuccessful approach to the competition coming from the Continent. British lager brewers supported their attempts by arguing that "if … we wish to retain our hold of foreign markets, we must bear our rivals with their own weapons by brewing their beer better than they themselves can brew it … [and] not allow our export trade to become the property of any nation under the sun without at least an effort to retain it."[63] Others brewers argued that copying the pilsner-style was not the correct strategy by saying that there was "better beer in England than any other part of the world, and it does not seem … advisable to go out of our way to copy those who brew beer not so good or well suited to our national taste."[64] This second argument brought focus back on the domestic trade and away from export markets. A lack of respect for lager brewers and lager itself underscored most discussions about lager in Britain. Those who commented upon the UK brewing industry's place in the world frequently ignored the very real threat posed by Continental brewers.

Until the mid-1880s, the best customers for UK beer exports were their own colonies around the world. British India, New South Wales, and British possessions in South Africa took the top four spots.[65] In other foreign markets, British beer had to pay heavy duties that made it too expensive for most

[62] "Our Export Trade," *Brewers' Journal*, 10/15/1875, 219–20.
[63] "Beer Brewing on the German Model," *Country Brewers' Gazette*, 8/19/1878, 372.
[64] "Correspondence—German Beer," *Country Brewers' Gazette*, 9/2/1878, 414.
[65] "Beer Exports from the United Kingdom," *Brewers' Journal*, 5/15/1878, 131.

consumers by the end of the 1870s.[66] German beer exports surpassed those of the UK in 1881, with Germany exporting 608,003 barrels to the UK's 458,319 barrels. Large shipments to India from Germany increased as British exports to its colony declined. In addition, new breweries in India were providing more British-style ales for local consumption. As M. Vogel declared in his article about the world beer trade in 1884, "The Bavarian mode of brewing … has cut the ground away from underneath the British beer trade."[67]

One reason for this loss of foreign markets was the continued insular focus by both major and minor breweries in the UK. The energies of brewers in London and the countryside focused on retaining existing market share with their popular beer styles of porter, mild sweet ales, and stouts.[68] Even as industry journals touted the strengths of the UK brewing industry or warned of the loss of foreign markets, UK brewers focused on building up their tied house systems to assure domestic consumption of their products without realizing the benefits of the export trade like the other major industries of the British Empire. By holding onto traditional national markets and business strategies including the tied trade, brewers of the UK lost out on the growing connections in the modern world of empire and trade.

Education and Brewer Training

There were many changes in education during the nineteenth century in both Britain and Germany, including the development of new curricula and ways of measuring learning in the natural sciences and humanities. These changes affected the brewing industries of the Continent where schools and laboratories worked together, developing a new scientific understanding of the brewing process as well as refining the methods and technologies in the production of beer. While the British breweries of Bass and Guinness established quality control laboratories earlier in the century, the training of new brewers continued to be done in the traditional way. Breweries in the UK

---

[66] "English Beer Abroad," *Brewers' Journal*, 7/15/1879, 184.
[67] M. Vogel, "The Beer Trade of the World," *Brewers' Journal*, 10/15/1884, 331.
[68] Gourvish and Wilson, *British Brewing Industry*, 144.

utilized a pupillage system that relied upon apprenticeships and learning on the job and disregarded formal education in chemistry and microbiology. In comparison, brewing education in Germany and elsewhere on the Continent was a modern affair that included the latest in scientific and technological knowledge as well the inclusion of cutting-edge approaches to business organization for efficiency.

Continental Brewing Education

Continental brewers benefited from several professional brewing programs that emphasized the use of scientific knowledge and technological innovation over previous traditional training that focused on only empirical knowledge passed down through generations.[69] J. C. Jacobsen of Carlsberg emphasized that in the 1830s, the Bavarian method of brewing was defective because work was entirely "rule-of-thumb" without any trace of theoretical knowledge and "guided by tradition handed down from generation to generation."[70] He argued in 1884 that one of the most important changes in brewing over the previous fifty years was a change in organization. He stated that large breweries needed managers to be in control and emphasized that the managers and assistants needed the proper education for running a brewery. To this end, he argued, managers and assistants should attend brewing schools to understand and produce an adequate staff of highly trained brewers and inspectors. Jacobsen argued there needed to be more access to proper brewing education, adding that "such further extension of brewing schools appears to be absolutely essential in countries like Bavaria and Austria, where the brewing of beer occupies a position of so great financial importance."[71]

As one of the few surviving early adaptors and supporters of Bavarian lager brewing, Jacobsen made clear that he had witnessed every improvement in the brewing industry as it occurred including the study of chemistry, vegetable physiology, and physics. Brewing, as he saw it, could only be understood as a

---

[69] Chandler and Hikino, *Scale and Scope*, 434.
[70] Jacobsen, "Brewing Progress," 109–10.
[71] Jacobsen, "Brewing Progress," 110.

succession of chemical transformations through the study of chemistry and physics and that "all further brewing progress must rest on special scientific research."[72]

As an example, Jacobsen mentioned both his own Carlsberg Laboratory, where Emil Hansen developed the theory and application of pure yeast, and the recently established Scientific Research Station for Fermentative Industry in Berlin. Arguing the benefits of scientific brewing and cooperation, Jacobsen foretold that "with this combination and co-operation of theoretic specialism with practical observation and experience, we have before us the welcome prospect that the further progress of the brewing industry will conduce to the general advancement of science, to the welfare and prosperity of the craft, and to the benefit of the community at large."[73]

Being educated in the trade of scientific brewing was popular not only on the Continent, but students from all over the world traveled to institutes like the Copenhagen Laboratory, established in 1882. The Copenhagen Laboratory was devoted to furthering the study of pure yeast culture and "alcoholic yeast" as begun by Dr. Emil Hansen at the Carlsberg Laboratory. The institute had become world renowned for studying the physiology and technology of fermentation and continued to graduate students of the science and practice of brewing ten years later. Between 1889 and 1892 alone, the Laboratory graduated 132 students. Most of these students came from Denmark and Germany, but several arrived from Norway and Sweden as well as Japan, India, New Zealand, the Philippines, Brazil, and Chile. The students took four courses a year and instructors taught in English, German, French, and Danish.[74] This was an international school of brewing, and the students learned the latest in how to brew the best and most modern beers. This included the most sought-after style in the world, the pilsner.

Learning to Brew in the UK

"Tried and true" remained the training method of British brewers. To understand this, ownership of the breweries must be taken into account because even as British breweries incorporated, the power remained in the

---

[72] Jacobsen, "Brewing Progress," 109–10.
[73] Jacobsen, "Brewing Progress," 111.
[74] "Copenhagen Laboratory," *Brewers' Journal*, 1/15/1892, 8.

hands of the former partners and hereditary leadership. Sons of the partners would be trained through pupillage and apprenticeship, mostly focusing on skills "at the copper-side" that they learned through experience, without theoretical examinations.[75]

The sons of partners needed to learn two essential skills: finance and how to use business connections. They needed to pay scrupulous attention to the economics of production and sales to maximize profitability of the brewery, and they needed to be excellent judges of character and develop their credentials via personal contacts with publicans, dealers, and merchants.[76] Without attention to modern science or technology, the sons assimilated into the family brewery and eventually into a partnership of their own either dealing with the malt and hop departments, brewing, or sales and distribution. There was almost no other way for a person to gain a brewing partnership other than through inheritance and connections.[77]

The management of British breweries was divided between "gentlemen" who were the sons of founding fathers and "players" who were salaried and rose through their own ability. Players were usually educated through apprenticeships if they were involved with direct production or articled clerks if involved with accounting or finance and were not formally educated in management.[78] Though gentlemen usually attended Oxford or Cambridge, the purpose of the university was "less to search for knowledge and more ... to be 'a nursery for gentlemen, statesmen, and administrators.'"[79] Overall, British brewing enterprises were slow in responding to the needs of the industry by not investing in the generation of scientific information or graduating trained managers, which allowed Continental brewers to get ahead in production quality and quantity.[80]

Even though the notable brewing scholar Dr. Charles Graham declared British brewing methods to be as good as Pasteur's new methods in 1874, he did call for a British "Brewers' Society" or "Brewers' Institute" that would have

---

[75] Gourvish and Wilson, *British Brewing Industry*, 244.
[76] Gourvish and Wilson, *British Brewing Industry*, 244–5.
[77] Gourvish and Wilson, *British Brewing Industry*, 244–5.
[78] Chandler and Hikino, *Scale and Scope*, 291.
[79] Chandler and Hikino, *Scale and Scope*, 292.
[80] Chandler and Hikino, *Scale and Scope*, 292.

a chemistry laboratory and a library to study the science of brewing.[81] His calls went unheeded and more than fifteen years later the brewing literature also called for the modernization of brewers' training by saying that British brewers needed to know more about science. In an article about "Brewers' Continental Excursions," the *Brewers' Journal* brought up the numerous institutions conducting research in connection with brewing including the Carlsberg Laboratory in Denmark and the Pasteur Institute in France as well as many of the brewing schools in Germany and Austria.[82] However, as with more modern approaches to science and technology, the brewers of the UK were slow to change their training and management of the brewing industry.

Conclusion

Continental breweries and those of the UK had different approaches to business management, exportation, and education. Similar to the choices regarding science and technology in the previous chapter, the breweries of the UK were not eager to make changes in how they did business or made their products. The strength of the domestic market and their focus on retaining market shares through the control of distribution remained the primary motivation for British brewing firms. Their failure to invest in distribution, production, and management slowed their growth to the point that when they finally desired to regain their overseas markets it was too late. In 1916, Allsopp and Sons Brewery out of Burton-on-Trent sent a letter to the Right Honorable Bonar Law, M. P. of the House of Commons regarding the German and Austrian's "large and valuable" lager beer trade in the British colonies of India, Australia, and the Straits Settlements. They requested government intervention in helping them recapture "markets which rightfully belong to them." However, the response from Cutler, Palmer and Co. of Bombay, Lahore, Calcutta, and London, was that "light beer" had captured the whole Indian market and was sold cheaper than Allsopp's beers. They noted that while

---

[81] Dr. Graham, "The Beer of the Future," *Brewers' Journal*, 3/15/1874, 68.
[82] "Brewers' Continental Excursions," *Brewers' Journal*, 6/15/1890, 361.

Allsopp's British beer "will undoubtedly always secure a certain percentage of the Market [because it is British], it cannot stand against an item such as this at the price."[83] The British brewers had lost their window of opportunity and were unable to correct their mistakes soon enough.

In contrast, Continental brewers sought out and utilized the investment opportunities of incorporation while pushing to gain new markets overseas. In order to produce an exceptional product and do so as efficiently as possible, they advocated and supported structured education for people in the brewing industry, from managers to brewing assistants. With their success in the three-pronged approach to invest in production facilities, distribution networks, and personnel they were able to overtake and surpass the British brewing firms and help spread the pilsner-style across the globe.

---

[83] "British Trade in Lager Beer," PRO, CO 323/734/22.

4

Where the Beer Flowed: Migrations and Markets

Introduction

By the 1880s, bottom fermentation and the pilsner-style had effectively become the form and style of beer brewing on the Continent. As J. C. Jacobsen of Carlsberg Brewery said: "A natural consequence of the improvement in beer has been that beer-consumption and the area of beer-production have greatly enlarged wherever the Bavarian system has been adopted."[1] As covered earlier this was due to how the Continental brewers, across national lines, worked together through their collaboration and adoption of new technology and the latest scientific discoveries with financial and institutional support through LLCs and formal education. By this time though, the pilsner and the necessary brewing knowledge and investment had already leaked out of Europe via European, and especially German, migration to far reaching parts of the world. This chapter will examine the role of German migration in spreading these light golden lagers from the revolutions of 1848 and 1849 in Europe to the shores of North and South America, China, and Japan. In addition, we will look at how German imperial conquests in Africa supported the spread of the pilsner both in their colonies and the surrounding regions. The following chapter will examine the somewhat surprising role of the British themselves, and the vast British Empire of the late nineteenth century, in supporting the growing dominance of the pilsner across the imperial boundaries that defined the era.

---

[1] J. C. Jacobsen, "Brewing Progress in the Last Fifty Years," *Brewers' Journal*, 3/15/1885, 109–10.

There were many motivations for German migrations out of Europe to settle elsewhere though the revolutions of late 1840s were among the most important in the early expansion of this style of beer. Even as they found themselves far away from their homeland, Germans gathered in new immigrant communities like many other diasporas. One very important way they helped establish these new communities, was through the shared experience of drinking their favorite beers, light and golden lagers. Following soon after settling in locations as different and far apart as Shanghai to Buenos Aires, there were lager breweries constructed and lager beers being produced and consumed for the local population.

This chapter is divided into two sections, one that explores the migrations of German settlers during the first half of the nineteenth century and then the last quarter of the century when Germany had consolidated under Prussian rule and sought to make itself a colonial empire in China and Sub-Saharan Africa. Both eras involved large numbers of Germans leaving Europe to either begin new lives or conquer lands new to them for the glory of their new empire. Both eras also saw the increase of the lager beer trade from Germany outwards to new regions of the world and eventually the establishment of local lager breweries producing pilsner beer. Sometimes with surprising results for the Germans, the Americans, and the British.

Part I: Revolutions and Migrations

Though the consolidation of Germany into a single nation-state would not occur until 1871, there was still a recognizable German identity for the region with many emigrants joining fellow "Germans" in places abroad, brought together through their similarity of language, culture, backgrounds, and a shared love of the exceptionally popular "Bavarian" lager-style of beer that, at the time, was still very overshadowed by British-style ales throughout the world. Many Germans, as I will refer to emigrants from any region of what became the nation-state of Germany, left their homeland even before the failed revolutions of 1848 due to many hopes of better lives outside of Europe.

Around 1830, the largest group of Germans in the nineteenth century prior to 1848 left the region. This was partly due to attempted revolutions in Europe that year but also because of the promise of economic advantages across the Atlantic Ocean. Throughout the 1830s, Germans left for the United States, from 10,000 or more in 1832 to around 24,000 by 1837 with farmers heading toward the Mississippi Valley and journeyman apprentices heading to urban areas to practice their mechanical trades.[2] Many more Germans would leave after 1848, however, and they would go not only to North America but also to Central and South America as well as to the British colony of Australia.

The European revolutions of 1848 and 1849 began in February of 1848 with revolts in Paris against the feudal privileges and autocratic authority of the monarchy.[3] Nationalist revolts in Austria-Hungry by Hungarians, Bohemians, and Italians also began with street fighting by workers and students in Vienna and a Pan Slavic Congress in Prague. In Germany, people also revolted against the Old Regime of agrarian feudalism and the oppressive police state that kept people under surveillance. The revolt began in March 1848 with an overwhelming mob in Berlin succeeding in forcing the King of Prussia to promise a constitution and parliament. This success led to the new Frankfurt Parliament convening in May just a few months later.[4]

There were many motivations for these revolutions that spread across Continental Europe so rapidly, and not just the motivation for human rights and freedoms with more participatory democratic governments. Economic motivations, driven by increasing industrialization and rising unemployment and crop failures, were also key reasons for the revolts as well as for the increasing out-migration from Central and Western Europe.[5] Between 1845 and 1847, prices for many important goods went up considerably with potato prices going up 48 percent, wheat up 250 percent, and the key ingredient for brewing beer, barley, rising 300 percent. With the feudal system still in place, peasants who produced the crops still had to deliver part of their harvests to landlords or churches, on whose land they had to work.[6] With the winter of 1847–8 being especially severe, the emigration from Europe reached new

---

[2] Carl Wittke, *Refugees of Revolution: The German Forty-Eighters in America* (Philadelphia, PA: University of Pennsylvania Press, 1952), 9–12.
[3] Wittke, *Refugees of Revolution*, 18.
[4] Wittke, *Refugees of Revolution*, 20–1.
[5] Wittke, *Refugees of Revolution*, 25.
[6] Wittke, *Refugees of Revolution*, 25.

heights. Though this slowed during 1849 when people were hopeful the revolutions were a success, when they proved to be failures, the migrations increased again in 1850.[7]

An important result of this large out-migration, especially concerning the pilsner, was that there was now German migrant communities spreading across the world and bringing their cultural and culinary traditions of food and beer. Prior to 1848, Bavarian beer—lagers—were only rarely available in the German lands outside of the Bavarian region, including even Northern Germany. Even then it was handed out in small bottles and drinking it was a luxury. With the movement of people within, and outwards from, the German states, bottom-fermented beers such as the pilsner became sought-after commodities. Even though the revolutions failed in changing the political and economic realities of the German and other European states, they did succeed in supporting the dissemination of these particular beer styles, with the pilsner being one of the first beers to be truly successful with the re-established monarchy.[8]

With the reestablishment of the autocratic regimes of Europe after 1849, thousands of Germans were among the many migrants who fled from Central Europe to locations around the world. While many of these were peasants and/or agricultural laborers, there were also artisans of various levels from journeymen to masters at their trades, and many who fled from political persecution for their support of the revolutions. Over the course of the 1850s, for instance, the total foreign-born population in the United States rose 84.4 percent with the German-born population rising 118.6 percent.[9] In Wisconsin alone the total foreign-born population rose 154.4 percent with the German population rising a whopping 225.4 percent. This reached a peak in 1854 before the rumblings grew of an American Civil War that came to fruition in 1860s.[10] While a bulk of the migrants from Europe went to the United States, as much as 90 percent of German migrants prior to the First World War, there were still over a half a million migrants going elsewhere.[11] With European

---

[7] Wittke, *Refugees of Revolution*, 25.
[8] "Deutsche Exportbiere," *AHZ*, no. 5, 1/15/1882, 36–7.
[9] Wittke, *Refugees of Revolution*, 43.
[10] Wittke, *Refugees of Revolution*, 43.
[11] Walter D. Kamphoefner, "Who Went South? The German Ethnic Niche in the Northern and Southern Hemispheres," *Social Science History*, Vol. 41 (3), 363.

destinations all overwhelmed with their own internal and external migrations, most places that Germans initially moved to, like Switzerland, ceased being welcoming destinations.[12]

Prior to the 1848 revolutions, there were already organizations pushing for German migration to Latin America and Australia. In the late 1840s, there were several societies devoted to exclusively to German out-migration. These included a society for Germans to settle in Western Australia as well as the Prussian Society for the Mosquito Coast that had support from a Prussian prince for an immigrant colony along the eastern coast Central America of what is now Honduras and Nicaragua. A Prussian consul and many German merchants also supported and actively promoted the advantages of Guatemala and Nicaragua themselves. There was also the Stuttgarter Society of Chile and a colonization society for Southern Brazil with its headquarters in Hamburg.[13] The Emperor of Brazil himself, Dom Pedro, stressed the friendly reception that any Germans would receive if they came to settle in his country, as many would.[14]

Where these German migrants went, so did their tastes and traditions. This included their shared language, cultures, and beers. Just as the pilsner lager was rapidly gaining in popularity throughout Europe, with the global migrations of Germans due to the economic hardships and failed revolutions, the pilsner and the techniques of lager brewing began to quickly impact beer production and consumption wherever these migrants went. While lager brewing and these light golden lagers were initially tied to German communities, both as the primary consumers and as a recognizable German-related libation for non-Germans, this beer style came to be adopted as the national style of beer of other nations, including the United States.[15]

In understanding the expansion of these light golden lagers, we must see how such disparate regions came to gain their own consumer markets for the pilsner. By following the German migrations to the nations of North and South America we see how they influenced lager consumption and then local

---

[12] Wittke, *Refugees of Revolution*, 48.
[13] Wittke, *Refugees of Revolution*, 48.
[14] Wittke, *Refugees of Revolution*, 48.
[15] *100 Years of Brewing* (1901), 156.

production to learn how, by the early twentieth century, the British brewing industry had lost their influence on the global beer trade and how even their favorite styles of beer, all ales, also fell out of favor with a majority of beer drinkers the world over.

United States of Lager

We begin with the nation that accepted more German immigrants than any other during the nineteenth century, the United States of America. Lager production began in the early 1840s with German immigrants to Philadelphia, Pennsylvania and Milwaukee, Wisconsin. These were the darker, amber-colored, Bavarian lagers that we still see today with the Traditional Lager produced by Yuengling Brewing of Pottsville, P. A. and the Boston Beer Company's Samuel Adams Boston Lager. However, golden pilsners would soon be dominant under family brands like Pabst, Schlitz, and Anheuser-Busch's Budweiser. By 1870, Americans would be consuming 6.5 million barrels of lager beer supported by 970,000 acres of land for barley and 42,625 acres for hops. Lager production also supported 45,000 brewery employees in the United States by 1870 as well.[16] In its retrospective issue produced at the turn of the twentieth century, the American *Western Brewer* journal's *100 Years of Brewing* takes care to note that even though ale production was important in the past, it was superseded by lager production to such an extent that it was "as near a national beverage as any produced in the country."[17] This even led the German-Bavarian produced beer journal, *Allgemeine Hopfen-Zeitung* from Nuremberg to comment on the brewing competition between New York and Boston in 1878 as the brewing of lager beer drew more and more attention and popularity with American families.[18]

It wasn't until 1840 that there was any bottom-fermented beer, lagers, produced in the United States. In Philadelphia, the influx of German migrants in the 1840s led to a vibrant community that included German churches,

---

[16] "Consumption of Lager Beer in America," *Brewers' Journal*, No. 63, 9/15/1870.

[17] *100 Years of Brewing*, 1901, 156.

[18] "Die Bierbrauerei im Staate Massachusetts," *Allgemeine Hopfen-Zeitung*, Nr. 27 und 28, 2/20/1878, 107.

periodicals and newspapers, libraries, singing societies, and beer gardens.[19] This initial nineteenth-century wave of Germans included John Wagner who arrived from Bavaria to Philadelphia in 1840, reportedly via a fast clipper ship of the era, with lager yeast in his possession.[20]

Though it would be a few years before an official brewery would be built, Wagner, who was a brewmaster back in Bavaria, set to his trade immediately with a boiling kettle over an open hearth in the rear of his house in the city. It was a small setup that could not hold more than a capacity of around eight barrels, and the beer was stored in the cellar underneath the small brewing structure to keep it as cold as possible while it was lagered.[21]

Nearby, a sugar refiner, named Charles C. Wolf had a local, "practical," brewer working in his sugar house named Charles Manger. Manger was given some Wagner's lager yeast and set up a larger-scale lager brewery of his own with Wolf's support. However, despite Wagner being the first, and Manger being the second to brew bottom-fermented beers in the United States it wasn't until Wolf hired different European brewer, Charles Engel, to work in his sugar house that the business began to take off. Engel had been a brewer in Germany and France before migrating to Pennsylvania in 1840. In 1844, with the use of Wolf's sugar refining apparatus, Engel brewed his own first lager in the United States, brewed with one of Wolf's sugar pans and then storing the beer in hogshead casks intended for sugar.[22] This initial Wolf & Engel lager was made only for private consumption though and was enjoyed by them, their friends, employees, and especially the surrounding local German population. Later that year, after a fire partially destroyed the sugar house, Wolf closed his sugar refinery in favor of opening a lager beer business and distillery with Engel called Engel & Wolf Brewing Co.[23]

For several years, Engel & Wolf could not keep up with their own market of the local German community which would regularly drink the brewery dry.

---

[19] Wittke, *Refugees of Revolution*, 13.

[20] *100 Years of Brewing: A Complete History of the Progress Made in the Art, Science and Industry of Brewing in the World, Particularly during the Nineteenth Century*, a Supplement to the *Western Brewer* (Chicago: H.S. Rich & Co., 1903), 207.

[21] *100 Years of Brewing*, 207. There is now an official city marker of this site that was put up in 2001.

[22] *100 Years of Brewing*, 207.

[23] *100 Years of Brewing*, 207.

Figure 4.1 Engel & Wolf's Brewery and Vaults, Philadelphia, USA.

Many times, they had to post a placard outside of the brewery to alert consumers when their sought-after lager would return.[24] Even as they expanded with their first underground lager storage vaults in 1845, due to the steady influx of Germans they had to rent out additional cellars in buildings nearby as their production rose to 3,500 barrels a year, or over 100,000 gallons.[25] Engel & Wolf soon expanded even more and bought up a new property on the Schuylkill River in 1849 where they excavated extensive vaults over 200 feet long for their growing lager business that soon has a new brew house, malt-storage house, boiler-house,

---

[24] *100 years of Brewing*, 207.
[25] *100 Years of Brewing*, 207.

office and stables, showing just how much demand there was for the new beer, especially for a brewery near a large and growing German community.[26]

As mentioned above, an important destination for German migrants was further to the west in the areas of Missouri and what would become the state of Wisconsin in 1848. Another master brewer arrived in 1840, Georg Simon Reutelshöfer from Württemberg, who set to brewing upon his arrival in the relatively small—but growing—town of Milwaukee with evidence that his first beer keg was tapped in May 1841.[27] However, it would be the names of Pabst Brewing Company and the Joseph Schlitz Brewing Co., founded in 1849, that would make Milwaukee the famous lager brewing city it became.[28]

It certainly wasn't only local production that helped in the awareness and enjoyment of these golden lagers. Expansions of the Citizens' Brewery of Pilsen helped the original pilsner brewery to export its own beer to the United States and elsewhere by the late 1870s with pilsners arriving in the ports of New York and San Francisco as well as Shanghai, China.[29] However, further south in Latin America, the German immigrants were also setting up breweries for their own local communities that would soon have national dominance as the golden lagers, and the associated industrial technology and science, made an impact. Lager beer soon came to dominate what had been near monopolistic control over beer imports by the UK with much of the beer going to Central America being produced and exported by German-American pilsner producers.[30]

Central and South America

As recounted above, there were many societies and organizations that sought to promote German immigration and settlement in Latin America. By the turn of the twentieth century, the top brewing countries would include Chile, Colombia,

---

[26] *100 Years of Brewing*, 207.
[27] Dave Olson, "Milwaukee's First Lager Brewer," *Wisconsin Breweriana Journal*, No. 1, 9/9/2020, 1–3.
[28] Pabst was originally The Empire Brewery, founded in 1844 and then Best and Co. until it became Pabst Brewing Co. in 1889.
[29] "Der Pilsener Bier-Export, New York, San Francisco, Shanghai," *Allgemeine Hopfen Zeitung*, Nr. 27 und 28, 2/20/1878, 107.
[30] *Southern Standard. (McMinnville, Tenn.), June 15, 1889. Chronicling America: Historic American Newspapers. Lib. of Congress.* https://chroniclingamerica.loc.gov/lccn/sn86090474/1889-06-15/ed-1/seq-6/, accessed May 28, 2022.

the Argentine Republic, and Brazil with all the import businesses in the hands of the Germans, English, or Americans. While German imports demanded the highest prices, followed by British ales and US lagers from Pabst, the local brewing scene was controlled by German immigrants producing pilsner.[31]

Brazil

News of new breweries in Brazil, and most anywhere, made it to the many national beer industry journals of the day from numerous sources including consular reports, local newspapers, traveling correspondents, and more. One example of this is from 1878 in Brazil. Rio de Janeiro that was ruled by the Emperor Don Pedro who, as mentioned, was welcoming the German immigrants from the 1848–9 revolutions and telling them that they would be received with open arms. In 1876, the German consular report noted that even though the quality was not very good—no mechanized refrigeration yet—the production and consumption of beer in Brazil were increasing notably, with Germans such as August Kruss beginning breweries in the urban areas including the city of Pernambuco, over 1200 miles (2000 km) north of Rio de Janeiro. The report also noted that the lower prices of local brewers were supporting the consumption of local beer over imported beers arriving from Hamburg, England, and Ireland.[32]

Beer from the United States was also in demand. While American spirits like whiskey were not as desired, the local *Cerveja Nacional* was becoming quite popular with the light golden "Logos" lagers being held in the highest esteem and of the same pilsner-style as those brewed in Milwaukee, Wisconsin according to a correspondent for the American *Western Brewer* journal. The goal for this American writer was to encourage American brewers to invest in exporting their lagers and push the English out of the market, just as they had already done in Chile and Peru.[33]

---

[31] *100 Years of Brewing*, 1901, 266.

[32] *100 Years of Brewing*, 1901, 266; "Bierbrauerei im Rio de Janeiro," *Allgameine Hopfen Zeitung*, Nr. 14, 1/26/1878, 70.

[33] "Beer in Brazil: The Demand for American Beer in Don Pedro's Kingdom," *The Western Brewer*, 3/15/1878.

Just six years later, the German beer industry journal *Allgameine Hopfen Zeitung* was sharing the news of its own consul in Rio de Janeiro that told of a large decrease in the export of German beers to Brazil as a result of domestic production. Even with new varieties of beer exported from Vienna and Munich, the local consumption was already turning toward local German-Brazilian products by the mid-1880s.[34] Other countries which also used to have strong export markets to Brazil, including Norway and England, also saw their markets begin to dry up in favor of German lager styles by the middle of the 1880s.[35] Some of the reasons for this are for the same attributes that helped the pilsner become the first truly global style of beer, as detailed in Chapter 7, namely the distaste for the higher levels of alcohol in English beer and the large amount of sediment in the bottles. In the case of Brazilian consumption, the British *Brewers' Journal* writers in 1885 argued that the Brazilian trade for English beers in favor of German and Danish lagers was specifically for these reasons and the English brewers should take note and change their approaches to brewing or they would continue to lose market shares around the world.[36]

By the early 1890s, these lagers were sought after across the world with breweries like St. Pauli from Hamburg exporting, with great success, to Brazil, Argentina, Chile, and South Africa with its darker lagers and pilsners specifically considered superior to others in these markets.[37] However, due to much higher temperatures even the better brewing and bottling techniques made the preservation of imported beer in Brazil and other Latin American countries difficult. The multinational makeup of the Brazilian population helped with market demands for lagers, pale ales, and stouts but the prices were generally quite high and out of reach for many inhabitants. As the local production developed and grew from the 1840s onward it met the needs of anyone who wanted a more affordable alternative to the European and American imports.[38]

---

[34] "Ueber den Bier Import in Rio de Janeiro," *Allgameine Hopfen Zeitung*, Nr. 112, 11/16/1884, 1328; "Beer for Brazil," *Brewers Journal*, No. 235 1/15/1885, 15.

[35] "Transport of Beer from the North to the South Poles," *Brewers' Journal*, No. 63, 9/15/1870, 188; "German Beer," *Brewers' Journal*, No. 244, 10/15/1885, 348.

[36] "English Beer," *Brewers' Journal*, No. 244, 10/15/1885, 392.

[37] "St. Pauli Breweries," *Country Brewers' Gazette*, No. 219, 1/15/1892, 13–14.

[38] "Brewing in Brazil, from a Local Subscriber," *Brewers' Journal*, No. 344, 2/15/1894, 101.

Even as refrigerating technology became more available in Brazil, brewers needed to import most of their ingredients from Europe, including nearly all of their malt and hops, and with much of it arriving in such poor condition that it could not even be used for brewing. The largest and most famous local Brazilian brewery of the 1890s was the Logos Brewery of Rio de Janeiro with large brew houses, cellars, bottling and working rooms, and large stables for fifty mules to transport their goods around the city and countryside.[39] The brewery utilized steam power with a fifteen horsepower compound engine to move all of its machinery, and a refrigerator to cool the wort after boiling. The Logos Brewery produced several styles of beer including a Brazilian Imperial Stout and Brazilian Pale Ale to imitate English beers as well as a Lager Bock Bier and brown Bairisch Beer to imitate the darker German beers. They also produced a lighter, cheaper ale called Simple. However, Logos was seeing more local competition in the early 1890s from German-style breweries.[40]

These new breweries were being constructed in Logos' home city of Rio de Janeiro and São Paulo, about 270 miles (433 km) south down the coast. Through heavy local and international investment the new breweries had the latest refrigeration machines and were able to produce the Bavarian lagers, though they were costly.[41] These new German lager breweries rapidly hit the German import market very hard with exports from Hamburg to Brazil declining precipitously from over 900,000 gallons in 1895 down to around 260,000 in 1896 and less than 210,000 in 1897. Brazil was "by far" the most important international market for German beer, according to the British *Brewers' Journal* in 1898.[42] By 1901, there were twenty-five breweries in Brazil, more than enough to provide for local consumption with most of them producing pilsners and other German lagers with brand names like "Bavaria" and "Antarctica" to showcase the importance of the styles' origins and clarity of color (in comparison to the ice of Antarctica) to the local consumers. The most modern, according to the American *Western Brewer* journal, was the C. Ritter & Brother Brewing in Pelotas that was enlarged to meet demand and

---

[39] "Brewing in Brazil, from a Local Subscriber," 101.
[40] "Brewing in Brazil, from a Local Subscriber," 101.
[41] "Brewing in Brazil, from a Local Subscriber," 101.
[42] "Production and Export of Beer at Hamburg," *Brewers' Journal*, No. 400, 10/15/1898, 891–3.

furnished with a Carl von Linde refrigeration machine from Germany.[43] With over twelve of these breweries in São Paulo or Rio de Janeiro, the largest by this point being the New Hamburg Brewery run by J. S. Amaral, the import market had little to offer the Brazilian populations of European, and especially German, settlers.[44]

Republic of Argentina

Argentina, also a destination for many Germans fleeing persecution and better economic possibilities, became another hub for local German beer production with breweries beginning as joint-stock companies by 1866 in Buenos Aires and in neighboring Montevideo, Uruguay during the Paraguayan War against the Triple Alliance of Argentina, Brazil, and Uruguay. The model for the new brewery was the Hamburg Joint-Stock Company and investors were very hopeful for success, even in the middle of a war.[45] However, much of the beer consumed until the 1890s, similar to Brazil, was imported. According to the Buenos Aires *Standard* newspaper, locals were quite thrilled in 1880 how Continental European lagers were "driving the English beer out of the Argentine markets," and noting that "the taste of the people has quite changed within the last few years."[46] The *Standard* goes on to say that Buenos Aires was even "becoming a second Hamburg" due to the influx of immigrants and the transformation of the brewing industry in favor of lagers.[47]

By the turn of the twentieth century, Argentina had reached a similar level of local production to meet nearly all local demand with several large-scale breweries operating with modern equipment with Buenos Aires being the center of the brewing industry with twenty-eight breweries operating there out of a total of forty-eight breweries in the country.[48] The pioneer for this industry was Herr Bieckert, who had arrived from Alsace in the middle of the changing

---

[43] *100 Years of Brewing*, 1901, 266.
[44] *100 Year of Brewing*, 1901, 266.
[45] "A New Brewery Company in South America," *Brewers' Journal*, 3/17/1866, 1.
[46] "The *Standard* of Buenos Ayres," *Brewers' Journal*, No. 176, 2/15/1880, 60.
[47] "The *Standard* of Buenos Ayres," 60.
[48] "Brewing in Argentina," *Brewers' Journal*, No. 403, 1/15/1899, 46.

German-French border during the mid-nineteenth century and founded the Bieckert Brewing Company (Compania Cerveceria Bieckert, Ltd.) in 1860, though it was sold to an English syndicate in 1889. Bieckert's Brewery was an early adopter of ice manufacturing in order to supplement the refrigeration needed for lager production and by the 1890s included five refrigeration machines, several four-story buildings with elevators and communicating bridges and thirty-eight cellars for fermentation and lagering. With over 500 employees and twenty-four wagons for delivering his beers to the interior of the country, Bieckert's was the largest brewery in the country. His most popular beers, due to his German background, were pilsners advertised as the "Queen of White Beers," a bock beer, and La Africana that was advertised as "the superior of all the black beers." With a nod to the German Reinheitsgebot, he also advertised that "no corn or other injurious substance" was used in the production of his beers.[49]

The second largest brewery was established by another German immigrant, Otto Bemberg about thirteen miles from Buenos Aires in 1890.[50] Quilmes eventually became the largest beer producer in the country but in its first ten years still had a large impact with its beers being sent not only within Argentina but also to Uruguay, Bolivia, Chile, Paraguay, and Brazil. The brewery had its own ice machine, power engines and boilers, and consumed nine to twelve tons of coal a day to meet the local and regional demands for their beers.[51]

Venezuela, Ecuador, Bolivia, Uruguay

Nearly all the breweries in these countries were also owned by Germans or by German-controlled stock companies, including the importers. In Venezuela, the breweries were built by German residents who had mostly arrived from Hamburg during the mid-nineteenth century and their breweries, including the National Brewery of Caracas, had been able to drive nearly all the foreign imported beers from the market.[52]

---

[49] "Brewing in Argentina," 46.

[50] Silvina, "Un paseo por el Barrio Cervecero: su historia en fotos," *Perfil.com*, March 8, 2019, https://www.perfil.com/noticias/arte/la-cerveceria-quilmes-y-su-historia-en-fotos.phtml, accessed May 29, 2022.

[51] "Brewing in Argentina," 46.

[52] *100 Years of Brewing*, 1901, 267.

In Ecuador, all seven breweries were only producing lager beer by 1900 with the first of seven breweries in the country built in 1876 by the German consul, George Hermann. Nearly all the machinery, including refrigeration and ice-making equipment all came from Germany as well for the production of pilsner lagers.[53] While Hermann started his brewery in Quito, the first brewery in Guayaquil was not by an individual like so many of these others, but by the local Guayaquil Lager Beer Association, a group of German immigrants who decided that their local German community identity was so tied to their national beer style that they needed to band together to found their own brewery.[54]

While Bolivian breweries were producing ales as well as lagers, all of the trade was in German hands. The first brewery was built in 1882 in La Paz by Otto Richter with six more breweries founded by other Germans by 1900. One brewery in Oruro was founded by a group of German settlers, Heitmann, Koch, and Co. in 1899 in Oruro at 13,000 feet above sea level. The brewers there had a difficult time dealing with the high altitude in producing their own pilsner and Kulmbacher beers as well as having to use llama dung as fuel.[55]

Most breweries in Uruguay were also under German management and used all German-made machinery. After the first brewery was opened 1884, the company expanded to include six breweries all under the syndicate of the Uruguay Brewery. These breweries were then updated in 1900 with the latest German technology, showing the continued reliance, and connections between, Germans in South America and those in Europe.[56]

PART II: German Colonialism in Africa and Eastern Asia

In the 1870s, after defeating France, Denmark, and Austria in a series of wars, the several smaller states of Germans, including Bavaria, decided that joining the Kingdom of Prussia in a unified federal state was in their best interests. King

---

[53] *100 Years of Brewing*, 1901, 267.
[54] *100 Years of Brewing*, 1901, 267.
[55] *100 Years of Brewing*, 1901, 268.
[56] *100 Years of Brewing*, 1901, 268.

Wilhelm I was soon named kaiser at Versailles with his Prussian chancellor Otto von Bismarck the new chancellor of the Kaiserreich of Germany.[57] While Bismarck and Wilhelm saw consolidation of their control in Europe as their primary focus, they also saw the benefits and motivations for overseas colonies and helped organize the Berlin Conferences of 1884–5 that helped establish a rules-based approach to European colonization, setting off what we know of as the Scramble for Africa by the European imperial powers.[58]

Scholarship on the German overseas empire is limited due, in part, to the limited reach and control by the German Empire over its colonies that they soon lost after the First World War. German colonial ambitions were never truly fulfilled and the Kaiserreich generally repudiated overseas expansion as one of its foreign policy goals. They also held territory for relatively less time than the more dominant and longer-lasting French and British Empires due to their later start after 1871 and more rapid ending after the First World War. However, for its relatively brief existence it did have a heavy, and also deadly, impact on the regions and people it colonized as well as with the trade routes and shipping lines it devoted to colonial expansion and support. Through these, a lot of lager found its way to its colonies after the founding of the *Deutsche Kolonialgesellschaft* in the 1880s.[59]

Germany gained control of few areas of Africa: Togo and Cameroon, German South-West Africa (GSWA) and German East-Africa (GEA), also known as Tanganyika. The dividing line between the Cape Colony of British South Africa and GSWA, after the Berlin Conference of 1884–5 was decided as the coastline between the Orange and Kunene Rivers to the north of the Cape Colony and much of the early years was spent fighting the local African nations for control of the interior of the slowly expanding German colony. When Bismark was replaced by the new Chancellor von Caprivi, the new goal was to gain and hold control of the land "at all costs."[60] Even though the European

---

[57] Jane Burbank and Frederick Copper, *Empires in World History: Power and the Politics of Difference* (Princeton: Princeton University Press, 2010), 350.

[58] Burbank and Cooper, *Empires in World History*, 315–16.

[59] Wolfe W. Schmokel, *Dream of Empire: German Colonialism, 1919–1945* (New Haven: Yale University Press, 1964), via–viii.

[60] Helmet Bley, *South-West Africa under German Rule, 1894–1914* (Evanston: Northwestern University Press, 1971), 1–3.

population remained very small the Germans still established several larger towns and gained control of much of the land by the time they were forced to give up the colonies during the First World War. Though, in terms of limited size, consider that the total European population was only 14,000 in 1914, was up from only about 2,000 in 1896 and ruling over an African population, mostly Herero and Nama tribes, of 500,000.[61]

The major population centers became Windhoek and Swakopmund and were made up primarily of German soldiers (*Schuztuppe*) and colonial civil servants. This was even as Germany was attempting to create a German settler colony with civilians establishing ranches and farms further inland, but dangerously closer to the Nama and Herero. State employees made up the major consumer sections of the towns though they received nearly all of their provisions directly from the German federal government and would usually bypass the local retailers and importers, hurting and slowing the growth of the local economy.[62] To support settlement though, a public railway was completed in 1902 and Swakopmund gained a connection to the British transatlantic cable with an extension to Windhoek by 1901.[63] These connections were very important because the colonizers needed all of their supplies imported from abroad, everything from material for the railroads, for building houses, building water works, rifles, horses, and of course, beer primarily from Hamburg and Munich.[64]

Drinking at the colony was a regular pastime leading to many piles of empty German beer bottles. In 1903, there were 137 firms and companies licensed in GSWA and fifty-three of them were exclusively, or at least primarily concerned, with the local alcohol trade with one drinking establishment per seventy-eight Europeans. By 1913, this was supported by local production with four breweries, two distilleries, and three Weissbier breweries.[65] Within the major

---

[61] Bley, *South-West Africa under German Rule*, 73.
[62] Bley, *South-West Africa under German Rule*, 75, 77–8.
[63] Bley, *South-West Africa under German Rule*, 131.
[64] Tycho Vander Hoog, *Breweries, Politics, and Identity: The History behind Namibian Beer* (Basel, Switzerland: Basler Africa Bibliographien, 2019), 15.
[65] Robert Gordon, "Inside the Windhoek Lager: Liquor and Lust in Namibia," in *Drugs, Labor, and Colonial Expansion*, eds. William R. Jankowiak and Daniel Bradburd (Tucson: University of Arizona Press, 2003), 123.

town, and colonial administrative center of Windhoek, there was one bar for every forty-one settlers. Basically, one-third of all business involved alcohol.[66]

In terms of brewing in the colony, the first brewery did not come about until 1900 with Rudolph Jauche's Swakopmund Brauerei, which sold "Bavaria-Brauerei Bier," named as such for the connections to the metropole even though there is no evidence he had ice or refrigeration machinery to produce good lagers.[67] It doesn't seem that any actual lagers were produced until ice-making machinery came in 1908 and then four years later the Kronenbrauerei opened in Swakopmund by Johann Heuscheneider and began producing lager in amounts large enough to displace German imports for the still relatively small population.[68]

This goes to show where the German government and investors were focusing their energies and their finances. While good pilsner lagers were being produced in South America by numerous breweries, by the time the first lager is brewed and sold in GSWA, its time as a German colony is nearly over. Without the dedicated investors and business ties between this colony and the metropole, in comparison to the connections German immigrants to South America had to their homeland, the brewing industry of GSWA never fully comes to a level that could even be compared. However, just south in the British South African colonies, two well-established and heavily invested lager brewing companies were happy to send their own South African-produced lagers north after the South African forces, supporting the British, took over GSWA shortly after the beginning of the First World War.

In spite of its rather short-lived overseas colonies, the German colonial enterprises did succeed in leaving lager breweries behind after their own power was removed, with Windhoek Lager a legacy of that era continuing today. Far to the east, Germany also joined other European powers in dividing up areas of China as well and gained control of the region of Kiauschou (Jiaozhou) Bay in 1897 and where German colonists would open their own brewery, Tsingtou, in 1903. While the effects of German colonization were important

---

[66] Hoog, *Breweries, Politics, and Identity*, 16.
[67] Hoog, *Breweries, Politics, and Identity*, 23.
[68] Hoog, *Breweries, Politics, and Identity*, 22–5.

and the breweries founded by settlers went on to be large concerns in the twentieth century, it is the trade of German lagers in areas not under direct German rule that had the greatest influence in the later part of the nineteenth century. Among the most important influences on the spread of pilsner beer throughout Asia was the adoption of German lager brewing by the Japanese, who would soon have an increasingly large influence over the beer markets of China, French Indochina, and British India.

Japan

After the collapse of the Tokugawa shogunate in 1867, the following years of the Meiji era were ones of greater trade and more open diplomatic relations with Western countries by Japan and due to the efforts of Western brewers from the United States, Great Britain, the Netherlands, and Germany, many wealthy Japanese citizens were tasting beer for the first time.[69] As popularity for western-style beers increased among the wealthy Japanese consumers the demand to develop a local brewing industry grew with the first brewery opening as a foreigners' private brewery in Yokohama in 1869 that eventually became the well-established international beverage and brewing company, Kirin.

Due to the high price of imported beer, some foreigners decided to brew their own in Japan, including a Norwegian named William Copeland who had moved from Norway to the United States in the 1850s when he was younger. It was only after he had apprenticed under a German master brewer in his home country, he arrived in Yokohama, Japan in 1864 and soon opened his own Spring Valley Brewery in 1869 with three branded beers: Lager Beer, Bavarian Beer, and Bavarian Bock Beer, thus establishing the first lager brewery in Japan, or even in Eastern Asia.[70] He had a strong influence on the burgeoning Japanese brewing industry with apprentices of his establishing the first brewery in Kōfu in 1873. Not long after another brewing company emerged as the Japan

---

[69] Jeffrey Alexander, *Brewed in Japan: The Evolution of the Japanese Beer Industry* (Vancouver, BC: University of British Columbia Press, 2013), 6.

[70] Alexander, *Brewed in Japan*, 12–13.

Brewery Co. Ltd, which opened another lager brewery equipped with German machinery and managed by a German brewer in 1889 near Tokyo with others planned in Tokyo and Osaka as well.[71] It was to the Japan Brewery Company that William Copeland sold his own concern when he fell on hard times. Soon, in 1907, the Japan Brewery Company would become Kirin Brewery Company, Ltd, today one of the largest beer and beverage companies in the world.[72]

The Japanese government also took a considerable interest in this new industry and set out to be active in its development. Even though the Meiji era was one of more openness, it was still very difficult for Japanese to found manufacturing companies of any sort with Westerners, or any foreigners. The second brewery after Copeland's was established as part of a government directed industrial development plan for Hokkaido in 1876 and followed a specific brewery design for a specific style of beer, lager.[73] This new government-supported brewery was named Sapporo and much of the popularity of the young beer brewing industry was dependent on the prestige of the European heritage of this specific style of beer, including its adherence to the processes of brewing, the tradition of the *Reinheitsgebot*, and the decisive use of quality ingredients, most of which could not be found in Japan itself.[74] Local brewers were stubborn and insisted on importing their ingredients—the hops, malted barley, and even many of their brew masters—from Europe, especially Germany, which made certain that the definitive style of beer for Japan would be what they considered a traditional light German lager, the pilsner.[75]

Japanese brewers were even sent to Germany to undergo their training and returned with very Continental ideas about brewing. This included plans in 1878 to establish a brewing school in Japan to train young Japanese brewers, similar to the institutes that had been established in Germany. Natanawa, who was put in charge of the new Tokyo lager brewery by the Japanese government, had been sent to work in a Berlin brewery for three years at the Japanese government's behest in order to learn the trade.[76] Japanese newspapers were

---

[71] "Brewing in Japan," *Brewers' Journal*, No. 308, 2/15/1891, 76.
[72] Alexander, *Brewed in Japan*, 14.
[73] Alexander, *Brewed in Japan*, 6.
[74] Alexander, *Brewed in Japan*, 51.
[75] Alexander, *Brewed in Japan*, 7.
[76] "Bierbrauerei in Japan," *AHZ*, Nr. 3, 7/13/1878, 18.

reporting that beer brewing was becoming an important branch of industry in the country and the German industry press was taking note as Japanese papers declared that the locally produced Japanese beer was coming out healthier and more satisfying than imported beer.[77] These Japanese lager breweries were having a real effect on German imports. In 1887, Germany imported 67 percent of all beer into Japan but within two years, this rapidly declined to only 36 percent. The popularity of the pilsner was suddenly hurting the German export trade as local production reached higher levels of excellence with lower local prices.

The growth of the Japanese beer exports began to come to the attention of the British brewing industry by the mid-1880s. They had begun to see a noticeable decrease in British beer imports into the country as the consumption of German beer was increasing and even feared the cessation of the consumption of English beer at all in the country.[78] By the turn of the century, there were three breweries in Tokyo alone according to the local French minister and the Japanese government had even been promoting the consumption of local beer instead of sake through high duties on their traditional alcoholic beverage. The exportation of Japanese lagers, he continues, was even monopolizing the beer market of Vladivostok, Siberia and had made great headway in the markets of the Philippines, Hawaii, and the Chinese treaty ports.[79]

Conclusion

Even as Continental brewers were developing and refining their production methods through the latest technological and scientific knowledge, their styles of beer were already spreading far and wide across the world with the outflow of German immigration. As Germans fled poverty and revolution to the Americas in the 1830s and 1850s or followed the Kaiser Reich hopes of imperial power in the 1880s and 1890s, they brought with them their taste for the pilsner. Through the second half of the nineteenth century the export

---

[77] "Die Bierbrauerei in Japan," *AHZ*, Nr. 49, 6/18/1882, 411.
[78] "Bierexport nach Japan," *AHZ*, Nr. 27, 3/23/1884, 312.
[79] "Brewing Trade in Japan," *Brewers' Journal*, No. 418, 4/15/1900, 219.

markets for German breweries nearly dried up in the United States, Brazil, and even Japan as local production, by German settlers and hired German brewers produced their own lagers that utilized the same brewing knowledge and took advantage of the same sources of investment capital. However, by the turn of the twentieth century the pilsner had also reached beyond the spaces defined by German immigration and even included those who, seemingly, should be the last to consume and produce the light golden lagers: the British.

What the French minister above did not mention in his comments on how well Japanese export trade with beer was doing is how well these beers were doing in other markets, namely British India and beyond. For that, we now turn to how the pilsner came to dominate the most unlikely of places at the end of the nineteenth century, even more unlikely than Japan: British colonies.

For a nation that successfully controlled the earliest industrialization of brewing in the world and supported the early technological and scientific studies of brewing beer in the eighteenth century, it came as quite a surprise to many there that their ales were losing markets everywhere but in the UK itself by the turn of the twentieth century. Even as the British Empire controlled more geographic area and colonized more populations than any other European nation, the colonized and colonizers alike all turned away from the metropolitan styles of beer in favor of the light, golden pilsner.

5

Where the Beer Flowed: British Imperial Trade Networks

As the previous chapter shows, German migrations were important in helping to bring the pilsner to far-flung locations around the globe. This chapter will illustrate how non-German networks also contributed to the eventual dominance of this style of beer. However, to begin, we need to examine the geopolitical state of the world in the latter half of the nineteenth century: in other words, the imperial world fashioned by European powers in their search for wealth, influence, and power. Connections between colonies and European metropoles were essential to the survival of colonies and to the maintenance of colonial dominance. Of course, trade went both ways: while colonies provided cash crops and raw materials, Europe provided the colonies with food, finished goods and supplies, and—crucially for this story—beer.

By the end of the nineteenth century, much of the world had been effectively divided between the European powers, especially the British and French and to a lesser extent, the Germans and Dutch with some Spanish and Portuguese colonies remaining as well. While much has been written about the more direct colonial-metropole relationships of each European nation, there were also overlapping trades between different colonies and colonial powers and it is through these that one nation's consumptive choices were able to spill over into another nation's colonies. This was how the pilsner eventually became entrenched in British colonies around the world by the turn of the twentieth century.

This chapter focuses on the history of beer in the British colonies of South Africa, India, and Australia. Beer was an important story in these colonies for many reasons. The British Empire was the dominant empire of the late nineteenth century and encompassed more physical territory and colonized more people than the other empires of the time. The British colonizers kept close ties to their metropole through trade and the establishment of British institutions in the colonies including educational systems, judicial systems, and political structures. For much of the 1800s, British colonists were drinking British-produced ales, regardless of their location around the world. However, by the turn of the twentieth century all of these British colonies were producing and consuming the light golden lagers typical of their German rivals: pilsners. The imperial networks of trade between rival nations and rival empires supported the spread of the pilsner by offering opportunities for new technology, new relationships, and new consumer markets that weakened the metropolitan loyalties between British colonists and their home country. As the colonial settlers from Europe developed their own domestic economies alongside the colonial trade with their metropole, they also included nearby colonies and settlers of other European nations. Their identities as British citizens and colonizers continued but became more complex as their new locations became a more central part of their identities, which led to different consumptive choices when compared to metropolitan British citizens. This included the decision by many to not only consume non-British styles of beer but also produce them. This included the pilsner.

Motivations for Imperialism

Money had long been a primary motivator for European imperialism. Money for the kings, emperors, empresses, and the growing number of gentlemanly capitalists across the world. The financial motivations for raw materials including minerals, timber, agricultural crops, and of course, other human beings, were strong incentives for individuals in the various European metropoles to invest in and support ongoing imperial conquests. Another side of this was also the development of new markets to exploit. As the European empires colonized, they also built infrastructure and urban centers as both colonial control centers and as locations to draw local, and European, populations to develop markets for the manufactured goods coming from the colonizing power's factories.

Local markets were made up of several groups of consumers. Initially most of these were soldiers or imperial bureaucrats but for settler colonies, these regions became the new homes for families, tradespeople, businessmen, and laborers. As the colonies grew, they developed into important domestic and international markets of their own and offered opportunities for European producers and investors to make significant fortunes.

Beer became one of these potentially lucrative products for the brewing industries of the imperial powers. Beer had some unique attributes, including its ability to link to national identity. Especially for the British, who claimed beer as their self-appointed national drink, their specific styles of beer and their early industrialization led to a true dominance over any other nation's brewing industry and local styles up through the middle of the nineteenth century, as we've covered. One would expect, as they did, that the dominance would continue into the far future. However, what they did not envision was the power of newer, perceptively more modern, styles of beer to come out of the nations of their rivals. Even as the brewing industry press pleaded with the British brewers to recognize the threat to their power and take cues from the Continental lager brewers to brew their own pilsners, they soon lost the colonial connection and export markets they thought they would always control.

Between 1870 and 1914, the pilsner-style of beer developed from a Continental beer to one with global reach in nations and colonies that had no direct political or economic links to the major lager producers. Each new beer market necessarily had its own story regarding the arrival and acceptance of this beer style; here, the examples of British South Africa, British India, and the British Australian colonies highlight the consumer choices made in a British settler colonies as well as colonies of occupation, the places least likely to adopt another nation's beer style over British ales. In order for the pilsner-style to dominate in South Africa (or any British colony), it had to triumph over well-established British beer styles, British brewing methods and British cultural perceptions of the lager. In other words, for the adoption of pilsner beer to succeed in British colonies, preferences of taste had to triumph over colonists' loyalty to their empire's own breweries and beer styles. What we see is that in the British colonies, while many Britons went to great lengths to retain a high level of "Britishness" through the purchase of imperial commodities such as cotton and foodstuffs, they did not do so in their choices of beer.[1] The break between British settlers and their country of origin regarding beer consumption is a unique element of the British colonial experience. In comparison, other European colonizers sought to replicate with precision the beers of their homeland.[2] In all of these colonies, the colonists began brewing beer as quickly as they could with limited materials and equipment and met with varying, usually poor, degrees of success.[3] By the 1880s, British brewing industry publications began, and then continued, to decry the loss of beer exports from Great Britain while at the same time the German and Austrian brewing industry journals happily pointed out their own rise in beer exports to locations around the globe, including British colonies. For British journals the writers continuously point out the changing tastes of colonial markets and that the British brewers would be smart to change their own products and production methods to meet the growing demand for the lighter, golden lagers. However, the British brewers generally ignored these warnings of trade loss and as one writer for the British *Brewers' Guardian* put it, "the German, Danish, and Norwegian brewers were the first to take advantage of our obstinacy in this matter." They go on to point out that the foreign brewers should be warned that colonial production was growing at this point in 1888 and the "progress of brewing in Australia, India, and South Africa are amongst the most remarkable events of our time." It is with these examples that we'll explore the phenomenon of how British colonial brewing transitioning from ales to lagers. In each of these British colonies colonial beer and brewing preferences went from industries based on British beer styles and production methods to ones dominated by the pilsner and lager production between the late nineteenth and early twentieth centuries.

---

[1] For more on this, see: E. M. Collingham, *The Taste of Empire: How Britain's Quest for Food Shaped the Modern World* (New York: Basic Books, 2017); James Walvin, *Fruits of Empire: Exotic Produce and British Taste, 1660–1800* (New York: New York University Press, 1997); Sven Beckert, *Empire of Cotton: A Global History* (New York: Alfred A. Knopf, 2015); K. T. Achaya, *The Food Industries of British India* (Delhi: Oxford University Press, 1994); Roy Moxham, *Tea: Addiction, Exploitation, and Empire* (New York: Carroll & Graf Publishers, 2003).

[2] Sabina Groeneveld, "'A hotbed of sins' and 'just like home' - Drinking cultures in colonial Qingdao (1897–1914)" *Alcohol Flows across Cultures: Drinking Cultures in Transnational and Comparative Perspective*, ed. Waltraud Ernst (New York: Routledge, 2020), 8.

[3] "Prospects of the Brewing Trade," *The Brewers' Guardian*, No. 418, 10/19/1886, 319.

South Africa

In most colonies, European settlers were quick to set up ale breweries early in the colonization process. For South Africa this was just a few years after the Dutch established their foothold with Cape Town in 1652 when the first brewing license was issued to Jan Martensz de Wacht on February 28, 1664.[4] While this brewery existed well before the British took control over the Cape Colony, the local production of beer remained entirely based on British-style ale production through the first three-quarters of the nineteenth century. Nearly all the beer production in South Africa was also limited to breweries within and surrounding Cape Town in the southwestern part of the country. It would take the discovery of gold in the Transvaal in 1886 to eventually develop a large enough market for more breweries to be established in the areas of the Natal and Johannesburg. It would also take English investment capital and American brewing equipment to begin the conversion of colonial South Africa into a pilsner-producing and consuming colony, and then nation by 1900.

The European-colonists in South Africa, under British control since the early nineteenth century, followed the British beer styles and industry decisions in the same ways as the metropole did for nearly the entire century.[5] The largest brewing company by 1890 was that of Anders Ohlsson who began his own brewery in the Newlands area, a suburb of Cape Town, in 1880.[6] Ohlsson's Brewing maintained prominence across the South African colonies into the early twentieth century but was slow to adopt the Continental European styles of production and styles of beer, much to his later detriment. However, from his start in the 1880s, Ohlsson sought to build as modern a brewery as possible for his local ale production and sought out British companies to design and construct the brewery. He chose a well-established company from King's Cross in London, Henry Pontifex & Sons of Albion Works, for this project. The company had recently worked on another brewery in Cape Town, likely the

---

[4] Eric Rosenthal, *Tankards & Tradition* (Cape Town: H. Timmins, 1961), 13.
[5] Malcolm F. Purinton, "Good Hope for the Pilsner. Commerce, Culture, and the Consumption of the Pilsner Beer in British South Africa, c.1870–1914," in *Alcohol Flows across Cultures: Drinking Cultures in Transnational and Comparative Perspective*, ed. Waltraud Ernst (New York: Routledge, 2020), 123–38.
[6] "New Brewery at Cape Town," *The Brewers' Journal*, 12/15/1880, 396.

Letterstedt Mariendahl Brewery, and the architects and engineers of the firm already had a good reputation in England for designing English breweries.[7]

In addition to Ohlsson's focus on British-produced machinery and brewery design, he was also influenced by the British perspectives on brewing science, preferring practical knowledge over the more Continental scientific approach. In fact, he sent his head brewer to England for training and not to one of the well-established brewing institutes in Munich, Worms, or Weihenstephan where his brewer would have learned the latest scientific approaches to controlling the brewing process and fermentation.[8]

But beer consumption in the South African colonies was already changing by the time Ohlsson's new brewery was completed. In 1883, the colonial government was attempting to institute a new beer excise duty and the resulting inquiry found that imported ales were already in decline in favor of "Bavarian style" lagers.[9] Though Ohlsson would not attempt any lager production himself until the turn of the twentieth century, there were others who would. These include one local brewer in Cape Town around the same time as Ohlssson was seeking to establish his very modern ale brewery.

Aware of the growing interest in German beers, Ernst Matienssen attempted, and failed, to succeed at starting his own lager brewery near Cape Town in 1882. He could not afford the necessary machines or space but would buy consignments of ice for about £5 a ton and attempted to ferment the wort at as low a temperature as he could, even without cellars or his own refrigeration machine. Though he claims that he would have had success even without the availability of his own refrigerating apparatus or lagering cellars, he put the blame of his failure on the rise in imported German lagers and not his own lack of finances and equipment.[10] Within a decade, however, there would be a lager brewery in the colonies that would install and use refrigeration equipment of the modern variety for production and aging, a brewing company that

---

[7] "New Brewery at Cape Town," 396.

[8] Mikael Hård, *Machines Are Frozen Spirit: The Scientification of Refrigeration and Brewing in the 19 Century* (Frankfort am Main: Campus, 1994), 217.

[9] John Steytler, "Report of the Select Committee of the Beer Excise Duty Bill" (Cape of Good Hope, Appendix II, To Votes and Proceedings of Parliament, 1883), line 494–495.

[10] Eric Martienssen, "Report of the Select Committee of the Brewers' Petition" (Cape of Good Hope, To Votes and Proceedings of Parliament, 1885), lines 649–727.

would one day dominate much of the world and even own the original Pilsner Urquell brewery in Pilsen, Bohemia. This brewing firm would be South African Breweries, Ltd.

As the gold fields of the Transvaal opened and drew immigrants from around the world, the growing city of Johannesburg had few brewers to meet the demands of the growing number of local and immigrant miners.[11] C. G. Glass and his wife, with the financial investment of the wealthy, local, Marshall family, began Castle Brewery in the late 1880s to produce ales for the growing population of the Rand region of eastern South Africa. The Marshalls soon bought out the Glass couple in 1890 but then sold the whole concern to two Englishmen.[12] These English founders, Frederick Mead and George Henry Raw, had founded the Natal Brewery along the southern coast and bought up Glass & Co. along with the trademark of the Castle Brewery, in 1892, which would soon take on the name of South African Breweries, Ltd.[13]

For the soon-to-be-famous Castle Lager to be brewed, Mead and Raw had to build a brewery that could successfully brew lager beer. The first steps were to gain investors, all based in England, and organize the supply of machinery for brewing lager beer at the Castle Brewery in Johannesburg by ordering an entire plant from the Pfaudler Vacuum Company of New York City, who also agreed not to supply any other brewers in South Africa with their equipment.[14] It wasn't until 1898 that the first lager was produced, however, after construction of the new brewery was completed and after difficulties of brewing at 6,000 feet above sea level were resolved. When it did open in August 1898, it was so rapidly successful that Anders Ohlsson even reached out to Mead from Cape Town for a collaborative working arrangement in 1899.[15] Though this project fell through and the South African War began soon thereafter, Ohlsson recognized the threat and opportunity of lager beer enough to start building his own Cape Town-based lager brewery in 1900. The

---

[11] Malcolm F. Purinton, "Good Hope for the Pilsner," in *Alcohol Flows across Cultures: Drinking Cultures in Transnational and Comparative Perspective*, Routledge Studies in Modern History ed. Waltraud Ernst (Abingdon, Oxon: Routledge, 2020), 130–1.

[12] Rosenthal, *Tankards & Tradition*, 109–10.

[13] John Shorten, *The Johannesburg Saga* (Johannesburg: John R. Shorten, Proprietary, Ltd.1970), 905.

[14] Shorten, *The Johannesburg Saga*, 907.

[15] Rosenthal, *Tankards & Tradition*, 128–9.

new construction was for two new breweries built on twenty acres of land and to the most modern specifications. One was known as the English Brewery and the other, the Mariendahl, was known as the Lager Brewery, further emphasizing the different, national, forms of brewing production.[16]

During the ceremony for laying the foundation stone for Ohlsson's new brewery, he emphasized the changes that had occurred since he began his first brewery in 1880. Ohlsson focused on the investment he was making in reference to the science and technology of lager production, pointing to the new concern as an example of modernization and a point of pride for the Cape Colony of South Africa, as they could now compete directly with the imported German lagers.[17] With local lager production succeeding in the warm South African colonies we see not only how the consumer preferences changed quickly at the end of the nineteenth century but also the influence of new technology and how Continental approaches to brewing lager transformed the region within a single decade.

India

From the first British ships of the East India Company there was beer being brought to India from Great Britain. But for over a century nearly all the beer that arrived in India from Europe were British-produced ales like brown ales, porters, and pale ales. The most famous of these in the early nineteenth century came from George Hodgson's Bow Brewery with his famous Hodgson's Ale that dominated for decades until it lost market control in the late eighteen-teens. Beer was considered essential for the British sailors, military, and bureaucrats both for their long journey from the metropole and for consumption once they arrived at their destination.

As early as 1683 in Great Britain the navy attempted to support the needs of soldiers and sailors by building their own naval brewhouses.[18] Colonialism

---

[16] G. Bagnall, "100 Years of Brewing in South Africa," in Supplement to the *S.A. Hotel Review*, February 1853, 7.

[17] "Ohlsson's New Lager Beer Brewery," *Brewers' Journal*, 8/15/1900, 457.

[18] Peter Mathias, *The Brewing Industry in England 1700–1830* (Cambridge [England]: Cambridge University Press, 1959), 201.

brought about substantial changes in beer rations as British citizens settled or remained in colonized areas for extended periods of time. As private brewers expanded in the eighteenth and nineteenth centuries due to the Industrial Revolution and a rising urban population, beer transformed from a product produced in local markets and at home into a commodity produced for the growing malt liquor markets in England and abroad. Beer exports rose considerably between the end of the seventeenth century and end of the eighteenth century. Total beer exports in 1697 were only about 9,000 barrels; by 1800 this number had risen to over 90,000 barrels. In the nineteenth century exports to India alone rose from 14,000 barrels in 1832–3 up to 259,000 barrels in 1859.[19]

As the primary shipping agent of the British occupation of India, the EIC provided nearly all of the imported British goods to the colonists until 1815 when the EIC lost their monopoly and free traders began to gain control of the trade.[20] The British occupation in India was made up of a very specific demographic until 1858 when India came under direct rule of the British Crown and more British commercial houses changed the British Indian population considerably. A vast majority of the British in India until this time were young male soldiers in their twenties and thirties.[21] Many civil and military officials supported this population of regular British army soldiers and made up a wealthier and more elite class drawn from landed and aristocratic families from England.[22] These men usually served tours of duty that lasted upwards of twenty years and a majority of the soldiers died while in service, usually of disease. In large part due to the unlikely chances of returning to Britain, many soldiers and officials settled down and established themselves in India.[23]

The British community in India did not adopt an Indian way of life, instead they sought to recreate the culture and lifestyle they had left in Britain through

---

[19] John Bell, *Comparative View of the External Commerce of Bengal during the Years 1832–33 and 1833–34* (Calcutta: Baptist Mission Press, Circular Road, 1834), 75; Ian Hornsey, *A History of Beer and Brewing* (Cambridge, UK: Royal Society of Chemistry, 2003), 527.

[20] Mathias, *The Brewing Industry*, 189.

[21] P. J. Marshall, "British Society in India under the East India Company," *Modern Asian Studies*, Vol. 31, No. 1 (February, 1997), 90–2.

[22] Marshall, "British Society," 96.

[23] Marshall, "British Society," 93.

recreating the entertainments of an English provincial town by importing the commodities they were most familiar with and made them feel more at home.[24] The Anglo-Indian elite had been drawn from "a section of British society that had traditionally sought professional employment" and allowed only "limited concessions to an Indian environment in such matters as dress or diet. In all essentials, Anglo-India gloried in its Britishness."[25] However, it was easier to import some goods than others. While fabrics and metal objects traveled easily across the oceans, the British diet relied on a number of perishable necessities. One of the most important of these that was very difficult, if not nearly impossible to recreate on tropical Indian soil, was English beer.

British soldiers had other alcoholic options in India. Rice-beer and toddy (distilled liquor from palm-sap) were readily available to the British in India as well as imported spirits such as rum and wine. Fermented or distilled Indian drinks did not conform culturally with the British desires for retaining their European lifestyle. Due to the inevitable deterioration of beer in tropical climates, it was typical to substitute spirits and wine for the usual beer rations.[26] However, these forms of alcohol were believed to be detrimental to the soldiers' health, both physically and mentally. Alcohol and venereal diseases were considered the "scourge of the British army in India" and linked to violent acts on the part of British soldiers. One of the efforts to try and improve the conditions of these soldiers was issuing them beer instead of spirits.[27] Beer was not only lower in alcohol content and thus easier to ration in bulk, but it was also considered the British national beverage and healthy for the body. Through the mid-nineteenth century, beer was considered a healthy part of the English diet as a safe way to hydrate, as a cure for indigestion, and as a stimulant for the body.[28] The problem with issuing beer instead of spirits was that British-style beer was not readily available in India, nor could it be brewed easily in the tropical climate of the region.

[24] Marshall, "British Society," 100–1.
[25] Marshall, "British Society," 106–7.
[26] Mathias, *The Brewing Industry*, 196.
[27] Marshall, "British Society," 94.
[28] J. Stevenson Bushnan, *Burton and Its Bitter Beer* (London: Wm.S. Orr and Co., Paternoster Row, 1853), 18, 31, 22.

There were many problems associated with brewing malt liquor in India. The logistics of beginning a brewery in India were not economically viable during the eighteenth and early nineteenth centuries when trade, and not settlement, was of primary concern. Though ingredients such as barley and sugar were found in India, or able to be imported, the tropical climate of India made it nearly impossible to brew good malt liquor even if the necessary ingredients and equipment were found and put together.[29] The brewing of ale or beer requires stable, cool temperatures for the proper attenuation of the yeast for the best fermentation.

An article in the *Times* (London) from 1853 entitled "The Export Beer Trade" reported that "there [had] been a great increase in the exportation of beer and ale on account of shipments to India and Australia," both British colonies.[30] Trade records reflect the rise in Burton exports to India. In 1832–3 Bass outsold Hodgson by 1350 barrels. Exports continued to rise from a total of 12,000 barrels in 1832–3 to 83,000 barrels in 1857 and up to 259,000 barrels in 1859.[31] The significant increase between 1857 and 1859 reflects the number of British soldiers sent to India during the 1858–60 failed uprising against the British rulers. Advertisements placed in the *Times* (London) emphasis this growth.

Advertisements from 1861 and 1862 in the *Times* promoted the colonial needs for the British ales. An ad for Allsopp's Pale Ale mentions that their ale is "bottled for exportation … in the most suitable condition for all climates."[32] Salt and Co., also from Burton-upon-Trent, included a note at the end that they specifically have "Ale for exportation."[33] This illustrates the acceptance in London of the quality of Burton ales for exportation to colonies. By this point Burton had gained an established reputation for providing exceptional beer through their development of ales for the colonial markets. Without the Colonial Indian markets Burton would not have gained such notoriety both abroad and domestically.

---

[29] John C. Weaver, "Barley in the United States: A Historical Sketch," *Geographical Review*, Vol. 33, (1) (January, 1943), 56.
[30] *Times* (London), "THE EXPORT BEER TRADE." April 13, 1853, 8, Issue 21401, col. D.
[31] Hornsey, *A History*, 526.
[32] *Times* (London), May 2, 1862, 16, Issue 24235, col. D.
[33] *Times* (London), May 31, 1861, Issue 23904, col. A.

However, even at this time the local British Indian brewing industry was starting up with ale production and the first breweries being build high up in the foothills of the Himalayan mountains. The first recorded brewery was built in 1834 by Mackinnon & Co. in Mussoorie.[34] The founder, John Mackinnon, even sent his son, P. V., to train at Burton-upon-Trent later on and helped in erecting the New Brewery, as opposed to the original, in 1896.[35] Not too long after Mackinnon's beginnings, another brewery was built in the foothills by Edward Dyer at a location near Kasauli, with his branded Lion beer, a British-style ale. He also set up breweries in Simla, Solan, Lucknow, and Mandalay.[36] His brewery was followed up by H. G. Meakin who came from an English brewing family in Burton-upon-Trent who purchased two of Dyer's breweries, in Simla and Kasauli before beginning new ones in Dalhousie, Ranikhet, Darjeeling, and Kirkee.[37]

By 1884, British India had twenty-four breweries that were concentrated near the colder areas to the north, with most of their product being sold to the British military departments.[38] In fact, just a few years earlier the British brewing industry press was taking note of a decrease in imports to the colony of India. They had observed that over 200,000 less gallons were going to the colony but that this was not due to less demand, but due to better local production for consumption. In addition, already in 1880, even with the local breweries producing cheaper and more palatable beers than they once brewed, the Anglo-Indians were "beginning to prefer the light German beers," namely, the pilsners. The author of this particular piece emphasizes that the British brewers should "take this hint" and start brewing less intoxicating, "cheap brisk beer."[39] Exports from the Continent to British India further increased in the early and mid-1880s by thousands of gallons, with the pilsner name mentioned explicitly.[40]

---

[34] *100 Years of Brewing*, 671.
[35] *100 Years of Brewing*, 672.
[36] Golden Eagle Lager Beer brochure, Michael Jackson archive, MJ/4/40/18—Indian Sub Continent.
[37] Golden Eagle Lager Beer brochure, Michael Jackson archive, MJ/4/40/18—Indian Sub Continent.
[38] "Ueber die Brauerindustri in British Indien," *AHZ*, Nr. 78, 8/10/1884, 922.
[39] "Beer in India," *Brewers' Journal*, No. 176, 2/15/1880, 70.
[40] "Export osterreichish-ungarischer Bieres nach Ostindian," *AHZ*, Nr. 5, 1/15/1882, 39; "Beer Exported from Hamburg," *Brewers' Journal*, No. 243, 9/15/1885, 316–17; "Imports of Beer into Calcutta Showing Progress of Continental Beers in Indian Market," *Brewers' Journal*, No. 251, 5/15/1886, 178.

Yet there was another competitor entering the Asian and South Asian beer markets at this time though: the Japanese. Japanese imports to China, Singapore, Bombay and other British Indian ports were increased in the late 1890s just as British India was becoming the largest Asiatic consumer of German beer and even as local production in India was beginning to offer some competition to those imports.[41] As mentioned earlier, according to the French minister at Tokyo in 1900, Japanese exports already controlled the beer market of Vladivostok, Siberia and were gaining significant ground in the Asia-Pacific markets of Hawaii, the Philippines, and Chinese Treaty Ports due to the high quality of the Japanese lagers, which held as true as possible to the German production methods and ingredients.[42]

By the onset of the First World War, with the Germans forced out of the British-Indian markets the Japanese lagers had captured the whole of the Indian market for "Light Beer."[43] Though there is no evidence of any lager breweries being built in British India to meet the local demand, there was apparently an attempt in 1908 by some businessmen of Calcutta to begin a new brewery that would import its own malt and hops from England and brew "beer, stout, and lager" at prices that everyone could afford.[44] There isn't any further evidence that this did occur though, with British brewers having finally made the additions to their breweries to produce lagers that they would export, including Allsopp and Bass from Burton-upon-Trent.[45]

Australia

Though the initial colonization of Australia by the British was supported by goals of creating a penal colony, colonization soon transformed the continent into a settler colony that sought to develop its own industries to support itself

---

[41] "Production and Export of Beer at Hamburg," *Brewers' Journal*, No. 400, 10/15/1898, 891–3.
[42] "Brewing Trade in Japan," *Brewers' Journal*, No. 418, 4/15/1900, 219.
[43] "British Trade in Lager Beer," Letter from Cutler, Palmer and Co. of Bombay, Lahore, Calcutta, Madras, and London to Allsopp, June 6, 1916, PRO Archives, Kew, Eng., CO 323/734/22.
[44] "Trade of Bengal: Calcutta Business Men Tea Companies Jute Interest," *The Times of India* (1861–2010), July 8, 1908, (https://link.ezproxy.neu.edu/login?url=https://www.proquest.com/historical-newspapers/trade-bengal/docview/234852369/se-2?accountid=12826), accessed May 31, 2022.
[45] "Allsopp and Sons," *Brewers' Journal*, No. 223, 9/15/1900, 526–7.

including hopes of wool and wine industries. From its first brewery founded by a retired solder named James Squire in 1795, ales were the only colonial beers produced for nearly a century.[46]

By the middle of the nineteenth century, Australia already had seven breweries that rose to ninety-nine by 1871 as larger parts of the continent were taken over by the British Empire and gold mines were discovered in New South Wales and Victoria. Colonial brewing, as in the other warm British colonies we have looked at, was difficult due to the warmer temperatures, softer water, and poorer barley than in Great Britain.[47] Local preferences in the mid-nineteenth century were also for lighter pale ales which were also much harder to make well in the colonies in comparison with the metropole in Europe. Overall, it was difficult to make a stable product and transport it very far without having it spoil. Due to these difficult conditions, much local beer was brewed and served on-site with most of the breweries located in the more densely populated Melbourne area.[48]

Continental beer exporters from Europe were hopeful they could make inroads into the Australian colonies in the 1880s as they sought success at the Sydney Exhibition that year with German and Austrian exhibits for lagers.[49] While there were English, American, and local ales also represented, there were over twenty Continental breweries represented at the exhibition that hoped to win over the local consumers. However, the main obstacle for them was the higher prices for these light lagers than for the British-style ales.[50] Local tastes were changing though and local brewers would soon take up the lager challenge for their own markets as British exports did begin declining during this decade as rapid progress by German and American lager producers put pressure on ales from the metropole.[51]

Brewing in Australia, as in Britain, was devoted to ale production for much of its early existence as a European colony but lager brewing started taking

---

[46] *100 Years of Brewing*, 1903, 669.
[47] G. J. R. Linge, *Industrial Awakening: A Geography of Australian Manufacturing 1788 to 1890* (Canberra: Australian National University Press, 1979), 311.
[48] Linge, *Industrial Awakening*, 312.
[49] "Deutsche Bier auf der internationalen Austellung zu Sidney," *AHZ*, Nr. 40&41, 3/11/1880, 161.
[50] "Deutsche Bier auf der internationalen Austellung zu Sidney," *AHZ*, Nr. 40&41, 3/11/1880, 161.
[51] "Diminution of Exports," *Brewers' Journal*, No. 257, 11/15/1886, 439.

Figure 5.1 Carlton Brewery—Melbourne Australia.

off by the 1880s with the Cohn Bros.' Excelsior Lager Beer Factory at Bendigo and the Australian Steam Lager Beer Brewery Company in Collingwood beginning to produce the cold, bottom-fermented beers in that decade.[52] The Cohn Bros. had started their original ale brewery in 1857 after migrating from Denmark during the 1850s Gold Rush.[53] Due to the Cohns' close connections

---

[52] Linge, *Industrial Awakening*, 314.
[53] George Mackay, *Annals of Bendigo (1851–1920)* (Bendigo: Mackay, 1912–26), 58, 391.

to Denmark, the brothers made frequent trips back to their home country where the Carlsberg Brewery and Laboratory was supremely influential in the scientification of Continental brewing through the work of Emil Hansen on pure yeast cultures. The Cohns likely saw lager beer both as a way to connect more fully with their birthplace as well as a good choice for their business concern and started Australian lager production in 1882.[54]

The Cohn Bros. were also quick to adopt further Continental brewing strategies including formal scientific education. Julius Cohn, who is said to have brewed the first lager beer in Australia, was trained as a brewer at the Worms Brewing School, a part of Worms University in Germany that had been founded as a beer-testing station in the 1860s, before becoming Head Brewer in Bendigo.[55] This was unique for a British colony to have a German-trained brewer brewing lager beers, but was part of broader connections between Australia and the Continent. Advances in pure yeast that began out of the Carlsberg Brewery's Physiological Laboratory in Copenhagen made its way to Australia by the end of the 1880s with very good results of secondary fermentations producing quality ales in Melbourne like those made in England, even though English brewers were not inclined to think a pure cultivated yeast of a single species could even produce a secondary fermentation.[56]

Another, still famous, brewery began in the late 1880s specifically to brew lager: the Foster Brewing Company. William and Ralph Foster moved to Melbourne in 1886 from their home in New York. In late 1888, they began setting up their brewery with the help of an American refrigeration engineer and a German brew master and were able to deliver their first order of Fosters' lager to hotels in Melbourne by February 1889.[57] The Exhibition featured brewers from all over the world, including Anheuser-Busch Brewing Co. from

---

[54] Wayne Tindall, "The Cohn Brothers' Story—Made in Bendigo, Cold Beer!," transcript (Bendigo: Bendigo Art Gallery and Culture Victoria, 2011), http://cv.vic.gov.au/a-diverse-state/made-in-Bendigo-cold-beer/the-Cohn-brothers-story/, accessed February 11, 2022.

[55] Tindall, "The Cohn Brothers' Story"; Hård, *Machines are Frozen Spirit*, 224.

[56] Emil Hansen/Alexander Miller, trans. *Practical Studies in Fermentation: Being Contributions to the Life History of Micro-Organisms* (London: E & F.N. Spon 1896), 242–3.

[57] "The History of Foster's Lager," About-Us website, (www.fosters.co.uk/about-us), accessed June 1, 2022.

St. Louis, MO in the United States, with many of them sending lager beer for appraisal, though Fosters Brewing is the only Australian brewery listed as delivering lager as part of the "Fermented and Distilled Drinks" category for 1888–9 celebration.[58] Also part of the Exhibition was a model brewery wherein brewers produced beer for consumption on-site. What is interesting about this model is that it was a model of a lager brewery for "German method of low fermentation," though using mostly imported English hops.[59]

Australian brewers also incorporated other recent brewing innovations and strategies, somewhat faster than brewers in England, as they attempted to overcome the difficulties of brewing in the warmer climate. From the 1870s to the 1880s, Melbourne brewers started redesigning their breweries more vertically to utilize gravity as well as support colder temperatures for storage below. Many also began considering the latest scientific discoveries and theories, including those of Pasteur, which all helped beer production in Melbourne by the late 1880s.[60] Even with adopting all of these other approaches to modern brewing, it was the artificial refrigeration that made it possible to control temperature in ways that allowed for the production of good, locally made, lager beer. There was one aspect of the British brewing industry that the Australian brewers adopted, this was the tied-house system of owning pubs that served only a specific brewers' beer.[61] These systems emerged, especially around Melbourne, in the 1870s and by the mid-1880s likely half of the serving licenses in the area were tied to specific breweries.[62] The Australian brewing industry managed to blend the two worlds of Continent and metropole, a perfect example of how imperial connections were not isolated from world trade and changing tastes.

---

[58] *The Official Catalogue of the Exhibits: With Introductory Notices of the Countries Exhibiting/ Centennial International Exhibition, Melbourne, 1888–9, opened 1st August 1888* (Melbourne: M.L. Hutchinson, 1888), 76.

[59] *Reports of the United States Commissioners to the Centennial International Exhibition at Melbourne, 1888, Published under Direction of the Secretary of State by Authority of Congress* (Washington: Govt. print. off., 1889), 137.

[60] Linge, *Industrial Awakening*, 314.

[61] *100 Years of Brewing*, 1903, 669.

[62] Linge, *Industrial Awakening*, 315.

Conclusion

As we have seen from these three examples, the British colonies were not only part of an important relationship of colony and metropole but also part of the global trade networks that European empires helped establish through their motivations of expanding their nation's influence and wealth. Even in the most unlikely of places, non-British styles of beer came to dominate the local beer production and consumption in the colonial markets of the British Empire. The well-established colonial ale industries could not successfully compete with the consumers preferences for pilsners, even after dominance for a century or more. With the development and acceptance of the latest technologies and scientific discoveries including mechanized refrigeration and the recognition of benefits of scientific, microbiological research, the production of lager in the warm colonial climates of South Africa and Australia was not only possible but was able to effectively compete against European imports. Though it took British India longer to develop local lager production for the golden pilsners, the beer drinkers of the subcontinental colony showed their preferences as the markets were dominated by German, and then Japanese, pilsners by the end of the nineteenth century.

6

It Tasted Better: Why the People Chose the Pilsner

Introduction

Scholars in a variety of fields, including history, sociology, and anthropology, have demonstrated that the choices people make in terms of food and drink are quite complex.[1] Choosing what to eat and drink is the result of many factors including the consumer's identity, matters of convenience including price, and concern over the consequences of what consumers take into their bodies.[2] Among the most important factors influencing such choices, however, is taste. This chapter explains the reasons why pilsner became the first global beer style in terms of taste. While the previous chapters have examined *how* the pilsner developed and spread through science, technology, education, and business strategies, this chapter explores the reasons people chose (or did not choose) to purchase and drink this style of beer over all others. I argue that the physical attributes of the pilsner—its color, clarity, alcoholic strength, and level of carbonation—combined with a perceived status as the beer of modernity elevated this style above the other beer choices, especially British ales. And as M. Vogel, contributor to the British *Brewers' Journal* wrote in 1884: "In

---

[1] Some examples include: Pierre Bourdieu, *Distinction: A Social Critique of the Judgement of Taste* (Cambridge, MA: Harvard University Press, 1984); Jeffrey M. Pilcher, "The Embodied Imagination in Recent Writings on Food History" in *The American Historical Review*, Vol. 121 (3), June 2016, 861–87; Priscilla Parkhurt Ferguson, "The Senses of Taste" in *AHR Forum in The American Historical Review*, Vol. 116 (2), April 2011, 371; Leora Auslander, *Taste and Power Furnishing Modern France* (Berkeley: University of California Press, 1996); Antione Hennion, "Those Things That Hold Us Together: Taste and Sociology," in *Cultural Sociology*, Vol. 1 (1), 2007, 97–114; Marcy Norton, "Tasting Empire: Chocolate and the European Internalization of Mesoamerican Aesthetics" in *The American Historical Review*, Vol. 111 (3), 2006, 660–91.

[2] Warren James Belasco, *Food: The Key Concepts* (Oxford; New York: Berg, 2008), 1.

beer, like in every other matter, the dictum of the great philosopher of our age will become a truism: 'The fittest will survive.'"³ Unfortunately for the British brewers, in most markets of the world, the pilsner was the fittest.

The pilsner became the first global beer style because it was cheaper and tasted better. While Chapters 2 and 3 cover the reasons it was cheaper in the long run, in this chapter we explore *why* people found that it also tasted better than other beers. Simply put, consumers found that it tasted better because it was new and modern, it was clear and golden, it was highly carbonated, and consumers felt safe from being too inebriated. The pilsner was imbued with the taste of purity and modernity that was expressed in the words people used repeatedly to describe it and how they explained its spread and dominance.⁴

This chapter is divided into three sections. The first section examines the physical attributes of the pilsner that were most attractive to consumers. These attributes include its lower alcohol by volume (ABV) compared to British ales, wines, and spirits, its golden yellow color and clarity, and its high level of carbonation. Part II discusses the reasons consumers in the UK generally refused to conform to Continental attitudes regarding "good" beer and surveys changing British tastes for lighter pale ales and the development of cheaper, low alcohol running ales as a strategy to compete with pilsner. The last section of this chapter brings to light changing tastes in a case study of the British South African colonies and why brewers and consumers there transitioned from British ales of the metropole to Continental and German golden lagers. Instead of the light running ales of the metropole, the Cape Colony brewers produced tickey beer, which was also cheap and low alcohol. The difference between the effects of tickey beer consumption in South Africa and the running ales of Great Britain was the influence in South Africa of Continental migration and a lack of metropolitan nationalism that focused on specific beer styles. South African consumers, who were not devoted to ale brewing like their counterparts in Great Britain, switched from tickey beer to pilsner as soon as pilsner was affordable.

As scholar Priscilla Ferguson says, "taste is notoriously untrustworthy."⁵ Taste, in Ferguson's view, consists of the most private personal connections

---

³ M. Vogel, "The Beer Trade of the World," *Brewers' Journal*, 10/15/1884, 367.
⁴ Jeffrey Pilcher, "Tastes Like Horse Piss": Asian Encounters with European Beer," *Gastronomica: The Journal of Critical Food Studies*, Vol. 16 (1), 36.
⁵ Ferguson, "The Senses of Taste," 371.

with the material world and, in its strictest sense, cannot be shared. In practice, however, many taste experiences can be shared socially, as they are when friends dine together, or colleagues have drinks with one another. And in fact, scholars have demonstrated that the social context of tasting can decisively shape the taste experience.[6] As a force in history, taste has distinctive methodological and archival problems.[7] Each individual perceives identical sensory stimulants differently. In order to describe them, one must translate them into shared language. Usually, narratives of taste inevitably draw on metaphors, but these must be set in historical and cultural contexts.[8] These narratives, made up of metaphors and adjectives are the taste archive that a historian may use when researching and explaining changes in taste over time.

The sensory perceptions of pilsner in regard to its flavor and mouthfeel, color, and intoxicating affect are how journalists, brewers, travelers, and local consumers all repeatedly describe the libation.[9] While the physical sensations of flavor may pass quickly, the vocabularies used to express them are found in the archival sources through the repetition of adjectives and phrasing or metaphors to explain impressions of taste.[10] The descriptions of Continental lagers and British ales discussed below point to clear impressions of a positive association with pilsner versus negative associations with British ales—especially in export markets.

Intoxication is inextricably linked to taste when it comes to alcoholic beverages. Intoxication transcends historical eras and cultures, and in many societies imbibing alcohol is a key practice in the expression of identity.[11] Choices in drinking alcohol are important in the production and reproduction of ethnic, class, gender, and local and international community identities. Regardless of location—Great Britain, Germany, South Africa or

---

[6] Ferguson, "The Senses of Taste," 371, 373.
[7] Pilcher, "Tastes Like Horse Piss," 29.
[8] See Pilcher, "Tastes Like Horse Piss," 29 and Pilcher, "The Embodied Imagination," 862.
[9] Mouthfeel is a term to describe the physical feeling of a beer in one's mouth regarding the body or viscosity of the liquid, the amount of carbonation, the possible heat that can come from higher ABV beers.
[10] Pilcher, "Embodied Imagination," 868.
[11] Jonathan Herring, *Intoxication and Society: Problematic Pleasures of Drugs and Alcohol* (Houndmills, Basingstoke, Hampshire: Palgrave Macmillan, 2013), 1; Thomas M. Wilson, *Drinking Cultures: Alcohol and Identity* (Oxford: Berg, 2005), 3.

elsewhere—beer drinkers sought out lightly colored, lower alcohol, cheaper beer at the end of the nineteenth century. The British had running ales, Germans had pilsner, and South Africa had tickey ale and then pilsner. The reasons for this include the different environments. While some may say a chilled, sparkling lager is more refreshing in tropical locations than in a cooler, foggy pub in London, this did not stop other northern Europeans including the Germans and Danish from seeking it out, nor did it stop the metropolitan British preference from changing to running ales from porters and even bitters.

A number of changes occurred between 1870 and 1914 that had an effect on people's drinking habits. As the Technological Revolution moved forward, people spent more money on leisure pursuits and other forms of consumer spending and beer began losing its central role in working-class existence.[12] After 1880 in Britain, as wages increased, consumption lowered, likely due to working-class males looking outside of the pub for leisure activities including music halls, cheap manufactured goods, and sports.[13] Improved bottling of beer had an important effect on where people consumed beer as well, making it easier to imbibe away from pubs. Instead of retiring to the pub, people purchased bottles of beer for consumption outside or in the home, changing the dynamic of alcohol consumption. Continental lager brewers happened to be the most successful in this regard which also helped in the expansion of the pilsner-style.[14]

In addition, those in power became increasingly concerned over social evils that the temperance reformers blamed on the consumption of alcohol, making lower alcohol beer an attractive compromise instead of prohibition.[15] After 1870, temperance propaganda was constantly in front of the public in Europe.[16] In Britain, this had an effect on changing the perception of traditional strong

---

[12] R. G. Wilson and T. R. Gourvish, "Introduction," in *The Dynamics of the International Brewing Industry since 1800* (New York: Routledge, 1998), 8.

[13] T. R. Gourvish and R. G. Wilson, *The British Brewing Industry, 1830–1980* (Cambridge [England]: Cambridge University Press, 1994), 29.

[14] Wilson and Gourvish, "Introduction,"; Richard Unger, "Dutch Brewing in the Nineteenth Century"; and Per Boje and Hans Christian Johansen, "The Danish Brewing Industry after 1880," in *The Dynamics of the International Brewing Industry since 1800* (New York: Routledge, 1998), 8, 13, 18, 61. Also see Gourvish and Wilson, *British Brewing Industry*, 45.

[15] "British v. Continental Beer," *Brewers' Journal*, 2/15/1877, 32.

[16] Gourvish and Wilson, *British Brewing Industry*, 38.

beer from one that supported strength and health to an impression that it was better to drink low alcohol running ales because they were of "light 'family' character."[17]

Regardless of the style of beer, mode of production, or size of the brewing company, quality of product was a key characteristic of taste used in the marketing of beer. The perceived high quality of golden lagers was promoted through ideas and notions of modernity and progress but was physically reflected in the consist qualities of the beer. Consumers of pilsner knew that the beer would be of a golden color, that it would have a low alcohol content, that it would be very clear with minimal sediment, and that it would have a high level of carbonation. In comparison, British beers came to be known for their lack of consistency.[18]

Consistency is very important in beer production, and for any mass marketed commodity. People want to know what they are purchasing and trust that it is what they expect. When they order a beer in a pub or buy bottles to go, they are looking for a consistency of taste when they imbibe. It was consistency in appearance, flavor, and mouthfeel that classified the best beer in the world at the end of the nineteenth century. Commentators frequently criticized the physical attributes of British beer in overseas ports including its alcoholic strength, the amount of sediment at the bottom of the bottles, and the lack of carbonation. For instance, in 1885 the British *Brewers' Journal* reported that British beer exports contained "too much alcohol, too much sediment, too much hops and too little gas."[19] This could not have been more different from the consistent golden pilsners of the Continent of the very same era.

---

[17] Gourvish and Wilson, *British Brewing Industry*, 38, 46.

[18] The Belize Advertiser, "The Beer Trade in Central America," December 29, 1888, BNL: MC536. The British consul at San Salvador comments in his report that the beer trade in Central America has now become the dominion of the United States and Germany even though the British used to have a monopoly. "He attributes this decline to the obstinate persistence of the British brewers in attempting to force an article upon the public there which is not appreciated any longer ... A little time ago an experiment was tried with a light beer, somewhat resembling 'lager,' which was imported from England, and the first arrival gave evident satisfaction, but, when shipments were repeated, the quality proved to be much inferior; the bottles, moreover, were badly corked; no wires being used, and therefore the beer fell into disrepute and the brand became discredited."

[19] As quoted by Richard Wilson and T. R. Gourvish, "The Foreign Dimensions of British Brewing (1880-1980)" in International Economic History Congress, Aerts Erik, L. M. Cullen and R. G. Wilson, *Production, Marketing, and Consumption of Alcoholic Beverages since the Late Middle Ages: Session B-14: Proceedings, Tenth International Economic History Congress, Leuven, August 1990* (Leuven, Belgium: Leuven University Press 1990), 124.

Part I: See the Difference, Feel the Difference: Physical Attributes of Pilsner

Remarkably consistent in discussions about the new lagers of the Continent within the brewing industry journals in Great Britain was the listing of its physical attributes that set it apart from the strong, bitter beers of the UK. While the pilsner's light golden hue came up frequently, it was the lower alcohol content that received the most attention. Under the title of "Odd Items," one article in 1866 reported that the keeper of a lager beer-saloon in New York City was arrested for selling intoxicating liquors without a license. In his defense he brought several witnesses who had drunk his lagers. These included an old German man who, when asked "Do you consider lager-beer intoxicating?" replied, "Vell, ash for dat, I gant zay. I drinkish feefty or seexty glasshes a day and it never hurtsh me, but I don't know how it would be if a man was to make a hog of himsel[sic]."[20] In other words, according to the German immigrant, one could drink lager beer all day without getting drunk. Beer that could be consumed in large quantities without high levels of inebriation were rare prior to the introduction of the lower ABV golden lagers, and this became one of its strongest selling points.

Low Alcohol Content

The lower alcohol percentage made lagers a ready ally to the temperance movements that swept through the western world over the course of the nineteenth century and, as J. C. Jacobsen of the Carlsberg Brewery commented, "good cheap lager appears to be the surest and most reliable means of combating the evils of alcoholism."[21] According to a nineteenth-century medical text on alcoholism (and referenced by Jacobsen in his 1884 address to the Technical Association in Copenhagen), people drank fewer distilled liquors in places where the largest amount of beer was consumed. Thus, in Bavaria and Württemberg, where people drank the most beer per capita, distilled liquors were going out of style as beverages of choice.[22] In Bavaria, he argued, "very few

---

[20] "Odd Items," *Brewers' Journal*, 2/17/1866, 10.
[21] J. C. Jacobsen, "Brewing Progress during the Last Fifty Years," *Brewers' Journal*, 1/15/1885, 30.
[22] Jacobsen, "Brewing Progress," 30.

drunken people are seen in the streets, and drunkenness is much less common there than in many other countries."[23] The Austrian Temperance Association (*Verein gegen Trunksucht*) noted that the consumption of spirits was on the rise in Austria in 1884 because the recently increased taxes on "good lager beer" made it too expensive for the poorer classes. Those with little money chose to drink spirits instead. In order for the lager to succeed in "its mission of an antidote to dram drinking," the Austrian Temperance Association argued that it had to be cheaper.[24]

British visitors to Germany also noted the lower alcohol percentage of lager beers, and the amounts that one could consume without becoming drunk. One correspondent of the *Brewers' Journal* who visited the Börsch & Hahn Brewery in Niedermendig commented that "you might take a good skin full of that stuff without any fear of being "run in," for although … you feel as if you had taken a glass of beer … the stimulating effect is very slight and you may refresh again and again without any evil effects. In fact, it is an excellent temperance drink … cheering without inebriating."[25]

Being used to the much higher ABV British beers, the reporter made sure to note both the temperance angle but also the amount that he could imbibe without losing control. Both the Continental and British brewers and consumers, such as Carlsberg's Jacobsen and the *Brewers' Journal* reporter, were well aware of the marketing possibilities of a temperance product and the potential popularity such beer styles could have.

Export issues regarding the high ABV of British beer are also a recurring theme in the brewing industry literature. Trade of English beer in Brazil in the mid-1880s was in decline compared to German and Danish lager beers in part due to the strength of English beer, possibly due to the strength of regional temperance movements and the tastes of German settlers.[26] The advice that was given was that:

> English brewing firms, indeed, would do well to look to this matter, since we are convinced that year by year the demand for English beer abroad will

---

[23] Jacobsen, "Brewing Progress," 30.
[24] Jacobsen, "Brewing Progress," 30.
[25] "A German Burton," *Brewers' Journal*, 2/15/1885, 79–80.
[26] Sönke Bauck, "The Anti-alcohol Movement in Argentina, Chile and Uruguay (ca.1870–1940)," PhD Dissertation, ETH Zurich.

grow less and less solely on account of its alcoholic strength, and tendency to deposit a copious precipitate; while the importance of this note will be seen in the statement that in a great measure it simply owes its stability to the large excess of alcohol that it contains.[27]

The higher alcohol percentage was seen as one of the only things keeping British beer from going bad in long transit, unlike lager beer that kept perfectly well with low ABV because of its brewing process and lagering.

The British brewing press ended up focusing on how much more Continental lagers could be consumed given the lower alcohol. In 1876, the *Brewers' Journal* noted that "owing to its exceeding lightness, quadruple the quantity can be consumed as could be partaken of in England without the risk of getting intoxicated."[28] Unlike British beers that were higher in alcohol and bitterness due to the belief that these were the only characteristics that would allow their beer to keep for long periods of time, the lagers were much less intoxicating and could be drunk in large quantities without heavy inebriation. British beer writers explained, incorrectly, that Continental lagers do "not keep well, its consumption … chiefly confined to places on the Continent where ice is plentiful, and where it is not the custom for families to have beer in cask at home, for a beverage of this light character can be kept on draught merely for a day or two after it has once been tapped."[29] The author was apparently unaware of the growing popularity of mechanized refrigeration in the 1870s, as discussed in Chapter 2.

Beer Clarity vs. Sediment

Another aspect of the pilsner that consumers focused on was the clarity of the beer. Due to the long aging process, bottom fermentation, and decoction mashing, golden lagers had very little sediment in both draught and bottled beer. This clarity was a very big selling point and an aspect of taste through appearance that appealed to beer consumers the world over. Beer from the

---

[27] "English Beer," *Brewers' Journal*, 10/15/1885, 392.
[28] "Beer and Its Consumption," *Brewers' Journal*, 3/15/1876, 73–4.
[29] "Beer and Its Consumption," 74.

UK, whether pale ales from Burton or stout from Guinness, tended to have a lot of sediment in their beer, a fact brought up consistently by consumers.

The large amount of sediment in bottles of British ales was a regular complaint. One British article complained that when the cork is removed from a bottle of British beer, it upsets the whole bottle because the pressure of the carbon dioxide makes it all "more or less turbid." The author suggests "we may as well take a leaf out of the journal of the Continental brewer … [and] store beer in cask for lengthy periods till no further deposit is likely to result."[30] The inference that Continental brewers were producing a better product through their lagering process, and that the British should do the same, however, did not affect any changes in British beer production.

British brewing journalists even used the lack of clarity in British beer, especially when compared to Continental lagers, to point out the lack of formal scientific education in the UK brewing industry. Lager brewers were particularly careful about clarity and made sure that no beer was taken from primary fermentation "that is not glass-bright." One British commentator said that the "ignorance of English brewers" is evident in the "supposition that turbidity of beer is due to the suspension of yeast" instead of the use of infusion instead of decoction mashing, because decoction sorted out inferior material that causes sediment.[31]

The British were even worried about the possibility of lager beer encroaching into UK markets and industry writers warned that "only by the manufacture of a really satisfactorily light bottled beer that the brewer can hope to stem the invasion of this country by foreign lager beer."[32] However, some expressed that by 1896 it was common knowledge that lager beer production was not profitable for British brewers even though lager brewers had an advantage in that the conditions of lager "brewing enable him to produce a beer that will not throw any deposit in the bottle and will pour out brilliant to the last drop."[33]

By 1898, the *Brewers' Journal* was declaring that modern beers were pilsner lagers and it was easy to explain their "universal popularity" because of "their

---

[30] "Defects of Bottled Beer," *Brewers' Journal*, 8/15/1885, 291.
[31] "Continental Brewing," *Brewers' Journal*, 9/15/1885, 330.
[32] "Light Bottled Beer," *Brewers' Journal*, 7/15/1896, 384.
[33] "Light Bottled Beer," 384.

quality, brilliancy, wholesomeness, and pleasant refreshing flavours that have made the beer-trade what it now is." They then delve into a comparison to the older styles of British ales, describing them as "thick, muddy, foxy, and unwholesome beers."[34] According to this English author, beer with copious sediment was unhealthy and a relic of the pre-modern brewing age. In comparison, the modern beer was brilliant and clear. As a result, they argue explicitly for clarity in modern beer, that "brilliancy is at all events to be attained, and that is a matter sufficient to test the quality of a beer [and] no cloudy or fretful ales find favour among the modern public."[35]

Carbonation

Along with clarity, a high level of carbonation was increasingly understood as a signifier of quality by both beer consumers and writers alike. High levels of carbonation, however, were a quality of golden lagers and not of ales produced in the UK.[36] The higher levels of carbonation came to the awareness of the British public after the Paris Exhibition of 1867 via the presentation of Viennese lagers from Anton Dreher's Schwechat brewery. It was promoted by the British brewing industry's brewing literature as being "both sustaining and refreshing." With the introduction of the Viennese lager also came an apparatus known as the "Automatic Generator," which produced extra carbonation at bars for the serving of this new beer. There was no doubt, according to the British writer, "that the provision of cool cellars and these carbonizing [sic] apparatus will help to solve the difficulty, which hitherto attended the introduction of the Lager bier [sic] to Londoners."[37]

An important signifier for pilsners was that they were "very full of gas" in comparison to the British ales and had a more pleasant mouthfeel because of it.[38] Carbonation was one of the key properties of the pilsners and according to

---

[34] "Brilliant Beers," *Brewers' Journal*, 10/15/1898, 747.

[35] "Brilliant Beers," 749.

[36] While artificial carbonation had been around for around a hundred years, brewers in the UK and on the Continent continued to usually use the natural carbonation that comes from yeast while undergoing fermentation.

[37] "Vienna Beer in London," *Brewers' Journal*, 7/15/1872, 197.

[38] "German vs. English Beer," *Brewers' Journal*, 4/15/1886, 123.

some it was not to be lost by taking ones time in drinking. One writer expressed that they should be consumed rapidly "if one of its essential qualities is not to be lost, and that is the carbonic acid gas."[39]

Constant reference to both "brilliancy" and carbonation is what the British used to compare British ales with Continental pilsner lagers whether in the metropole or the colonies. It was these properties in particular that showed the "true difference between beer of English and German production" alongside "the moderate percentage of acidity and alcohol" that did not detract from the pleasant mouthfeel and "by no means thin on palate."[40]

In spite of the benefits regarding the health and refreshment of modern lager beer as promoted by the brewing literature, the British brewers and consumers remained firm in their desire for British style ales. In addition to the strong preference for traditional technology and education as examined in Chapters 2 and 3, there was a strong nationalist reaction against Continental beers in the UK. Many British were afraid for their ales in the face of the encroachment of lagers. Many more sought to ease these fears by touting the strength of the British brewing industry. At the same time, tastes were changing even in the UK and brewers began producing new lighter "running" ales in response to the pilsner threat

Part II: Lager and the UK

It is difficult to reconstruct changing tastes in Great Britain during the nineteenth century even though those living at the time frequently made note of significant shifts in the types of beer consumed in Victorian Britain.[41] These contemporaries observed a distinct turn from the darker porters of London toward lighter (but still strong) pale ales between the 1840s and 1860s.[42] There were several reasons for these shifts in consumption, including changes in social habits and work practices, the impact of temperance reforms, higher

---

[39] Vogel, "The Beer Trade of the World," 334.
[40] "Pasteurized Beer," *Brewers' Journal*, 10/15/1890, 617.
[41] Gourvish and Wilson, *British Brewing Industry*, 40.
[42] Gourvish and Wilson, *British Brewing Industry*, 82.

taxation, fashions for particular beer, and small amounts of imported lagers from the Continent.[43] These shifts were slow to gain traction in Britain because British consumers still preferred the traditional strong, dark ales at home.

Some British scholars at the beginning of the 1880s pushed for brewers to begin producing "beer that by its colour, flavor, condition, and deficient alcoholic strength, would certainly captivate a large section of the beer-drinking public."[44] After spending time in several Continental cafés and beer saloons, Frank Faulkner, a British brewing scientist, frequent contributor to *The Brewers' Journal*, and author of *The Art of Brewing* (1876) wrote in 1880 that people there drank large quantities of beer but it was all golden lagers, pilsners. The volume of consumption did not surprise beer industry writers because they saw "its unvarying brilliancy and condition … a respect in which it differs so widely from even the best English brands." He explained that if British beers were to be produced with low alcohol content, it would be "washy, flat, unpalatable fluid, of no character that could be termed desirable." This was because British brewers allowed for cask conditioning that was "slow and incipient," which made it very difficult to control stability, especially with variable temperatures and climates. Faulkner argued for the British to produce their own lagers like those on the Continent but thought that "the system will not, I think, ever find a footing in England" due to the higher cost of lager production on top of the heavy duties they already paid. Even if cost was not an obstacle, "the majority of English consumers are so fond of the beer that improves by age, so proud of the fluid that will remain sound under trying climatic changes, that the weak, brilliant, and frothy Continental production would not captivate, excepting as a novelty, their critical taste."[45] And indeed it would be another two decades before any of the large British brewers attempted to produce Continental lagers, with no great success.

Faulkner pointed out the key attributes that Continental lager drinkers sought and enjoyed included the carbonation, low ABV, and "brilliancy." All of these features set pilsners clearly apart from the British beers which were

---

[43] Gourvish and Wilson, *British Brewing Industry*, 40.
[44] Frank Faulkner, "Principles of Continental Brewing," *Brewers' Journal*, 1/15/1880, 21–2.
[45] Frank Faulkner, "Principles," 21–2.

much stronger, darker with more sediment, and less carbonated. However, these distinctions of British beers were what made them so clearly British and what British beer consumers wanted and thought made their beer the best.[46]

By the mid-1870s, some British brewers began to express concern about the encroaching popularity of lager beers. One *Brewers' Journal* correspondent was "absolutely alarmed for the safety of the national beverage." In response to this alarmist, another correspondent wrote that while they "agree with his remarks as to the progress of the brewing industry in Germany and other countries" and are "appreciative of the efforts of foreigners" in the improvement of brewing processes, "we have no fear for the safety of the brewing industry in this country." Even though this correspondent admitted to a growth of German and French cafés in London, he argued that the consumption of Continental beers "is almost exclusively confined to foreigners … [and] chiefly in demand during hot weather, when its light character renders it an appropriate and wholesome drink." The second correspondent finished by reiterating that the original alarmist "has an exaggerated notion of the whole matter" and that the only reason he responded was due to the amount of "lively communication directed to us, in which apprehensions of the most unfounded character are expressed."[47]

This article brought several key perceptions to the forefront at a time of considerable expansion for pilsners on the Continent. The fears expressed by the first correspondent were mirrored by enough readers of the *Brewers' Journal* that the journal editors felt they must respond and assuage fears that British ales were still the most popular in Great Britain and that the national industry was in no way threatened by foreign brewers. The taste for lagers, they surmised, was a taste favored by foreigners rather than the British. Foreign brewers' presses, including the *Montieur de la Brasserie*, supported these ideas. The French brewers' journal pointed out that German emigration was the cause for the growth of lager consumption in Britain. The French writer explained that "these beers are consumed almost exclusively by foreigners, that they are drunk especially in the summer, when they are very refreshing, that in England, for the most part, they are only to be purchased at the foreign cafés,

---

[46] "German Beer," *Country Brewers' Gazette*, 9/2/1878, 414; Gourvish and Wilson, *British Brewing Industry*, 42.

[47] "Trop de Zele," *Brewers' Journal*, 10/15/1876, 224.

and that, so far, English beer has nothing to fear from this competition."[48] Local and foreign beer writers both tried to be clear that the taste for golden lagers was a Continental choice and one no English beer drinkers would make on their home soil.

The discussion surrounding the encroachment of foreign lagers in the *Brewers' Journal* continued over several more issues under varied titles. Each new installment, however, focused on the strength of British beer consumption over foreign lagers in the home markets. One of the reasons given for this came after a temperance advocate named Mr. Walker complained at a temperance event that "the English brewers did not brew a beer of the light Continental description," to which the journal responded that "it is not a question of supply, but of demand." The journal went on to say that "the majority of English beer-drinkers, for whom the brewers have to cater, would not drink German beer, it does not suit their taste, and, for well-grounded reasons, they prefer the native product." These reasons included "climate, temperament, and even physical condition which render it improbable that English beer-drinkers will be satisfied with the same kind of beer that is popular on the Continent."[49] Mr. Bass of the Bass Brewery supported the idea that the British population wanted specific British styles, not that the British brewing industry was unable to produce quality lagers.[50]

When asked by the temperance advocate, "why don't you brew a beer which will be pleasant to drink without making people drunk?" Mr. Bass replied that it was simple to do so and that he did regularly brew thousands of gallons of light beer at harvest time. Bass went on to say that "to day the brewers have no objection to producing the kind of beer [temperance] praises—perhaps a little unduly—but if people would not drink it, the experiment in these days of excessive competition would be very likely to have disastrous results for the brewer if not the consumer."[51] Bass's opinions were supported by a British pub owner, who wrote in to say that "we brew, according to my thinking, better beer in England than any other part of the world, and it does not seem to me

---

[48] "English v. German Beer," *Brewers' Journal*, 11/15/1876, 246.
[49] "British v. Continental Beer," 32.
[50] "British v. Continental Beer," 32.
[51] "British v. Continental Beer," 32.

advisable to go out of our way to copy those who brew beer not so good or well suited to our national taste," and that his "tenants would not thank me to send them a weak, washy beer, nor would they get people to drink it, just because it was brewed after a fashion of the German beer."[52] Furthermore, as a correspondent bluntly explained in 1877, "most English beer-drinkers object to the palate flavor of German beers."[53]

As this exchange indicates, the opinions at the close of the 1870s were that British beer was best and could not be substituted by any German/Continental lagers because differences of taste would leave the British consumers very disappointed and negatively affect the brewers' bottom lines.[54] However, British brewers did not ignore these calls for a lighter, lower alcohol beer completely. Instead, they turned to a strategy of producing their own response to German lagers: running ales.

The British running ales were pale and mild ales produced after 1875 in response to the growing pressure of pilsner.[55] British brewers produced running ales using the same methods as other ale but the end result was lower in alcohol, lighter in flavor and color, and could be produced quickly for a fast turnover in profit.[56] However, unlike the Continental lagers, these beers would not keep long and were never stored.[57] Running ales allowed the British brewers to retain their traditional methods and avoid expensive investment in lager brewing facilities while still producing a product similar to German lagers, at least in terms of alcohol percentage and color. In addition, running ales allowed the British brewers, and consumers, to remain loyal to their national styles and methods.

The loyalty to British traditions of taste and brewing was supported in the brewing literature in the early 1880s. In response to the promotion of lager in 1879 by an editor of the British society journal, *Truth*, the *Brewers' Journal*

---

[52] "Correspondence—GERMAN BEER," *Brewers' Journal*, 9/2/1878, 414.

[53] "German Beers," *Brewers' Journal*, 5/15/1877, 133.

[54] Richard Wilson, "Changing Taste for Beer in Victorian Britain," in *The Dynamics of the International Brewing Industry since 1800*, eds. R. G. Wilson and T. R. Gourvish (New York: Routledge, 1998), 102.

[55] Wilson, "Changing Taste for Beer in Victorian Britain," 99.

[56] Wilson, "Changing Taste for Beer in Victorian Britain," 103. The first reference I have found is from M. Vogel's 1884 article in a reference to Bass producing stock beers instead of running beers; Vogel, "The Beer Trade of the World," 331.

[57] Gourvish and Wilson, *British Brewing Industry*, 45.

argued that the editor must not have known anything about British beer or its consumers. The British brewers, he argued, must continue to "produce a fluid that will keep their plant in full work, a beer that will satisfy the wants of the working classes as a whole ... the lager beer is mere wash that would refuse to remain sound for many hours together, and would in no wise tempt by its virtues the English consumer."[58] Several years later these arguments were taken up by a different correspondent, who explained that English brewers were typically conservative and would oppose any future introduction of bottom fermentation systems in England. The brewers' "favourite can't [sic] has been that the alcoholic thirst of the British working public could not satiate itself with watery 'lager beers' ... To the Englishman drinking lager beer for the first time, the taste is decidedly objectionable."[59]

However, in the coming decades British tastes did slowly change toward lighter running ales for national consumption. As early as 1882 an article about the difficulties regarding different kinds of malt reminded the readers that the "modern palate likings are for weak as opposed to strong beers."[60] At the same time Professor Graham, a noted agricultural chemist and later a brewers' consultant, explained the British palate was used to specific flavors and that "English ales will hold their position for a long time to come since we have become accustomed to the alcohol and hops, and a change in the public taste must ever be a slow process."[61]

In addition, the running ales of Britain could not compete against pilsner outside of the UK. While the production of these light and cheap ales satiated changing British tastes toward light and mild beers, they could not be transported long distances to reach foreign markets. It was a strategy for maintaining national markets only. Though the British brewers recognized the trend toward lighter, low ABV beers, their reticence against Continental beer and brewing methods continued because of their loyalty to nationalist ideals and the belief that their ways were the best. As the contemporary literature shows, British brewers continued to believe that their beers and methods were the best in

---

[58] "German Lager Beer," *Brewers' Journal*, 8/15/1879, 242.
[59] "Continental Beers and Brewing," *Brewers' Journal*, 2/15/1882, 54–5.
[60] "Difficulties of Modern Brewing," *Brewers' Journal*, 2/15/1882, 52.
[61] "Export of German Beer," *Brewers' Journal*, 10/15/1884, 332.

the world. Even as fears were expressed openly about lagers coming to Britain there were many more voices supporting the idea of the strength of the British brewing industry and its beer. However, this was not the case in British South Africa where metropolitan loyalty was not as strong and the beer consumers readily adopted lager as soon as it was available and affordable in the late 1890s.

Part III: A Colonial Change: Why South Africans Chose Pilsner

While there are a few mentions of lager beer in South Africa prior to the large-scale production by South African Breweries in the late 1890s, there was a style of ale that acted as a precursor that was produced by local, Cape Colony brewers: the tickey beer. Tickey beer was cheap, low alcohol beer named after a silver three penny piece, equivalent to 1p.[62] Tickey beer was a beer style native to South Africa and produced by Cape Colony brewers in large amounts. The brewers made it from the second mash of malt, which had much less fermentable sugar, and which in turn produced a beer with much lower ABV.[63] This beer was essential to the well-being of the Cape brewers because while they produced standard British beers like stout, porter, pale ale, and export ale, these were much more expensive and most of the working class could not afford them. Also, as the keeper of a high-end hotel in Cape Town explained in 1885, when imported British ales were available and affordable, consumers preferred them. When asked whether customers preferred local or imported beer, he said they like "the English ale, although I have seen some colonial ale equally as good. As a rule, English people prefer English ale."[64]

In 1883, the Cape Colony Parliament began proceedings to increase duties on beer in the colony. The excise bill, which was passed that year, sought to raise the price of both imports and Cape ales. The Select Committee on the

---

[62] Rudyard Kipling and Jan Montefiore, "Mrs. Bathurst," Explanation of Terms in *The Man Who Would Be King: [Selected Stories of Rudyard Kipling]* (London: Penguin Books, 2011).
[63] John Spence, "Report of the Select Committee of the Brewers' Petition" (Cape of Good Hope, To Votes and Proceedings of Parliament, 1885), line 50.
[64] James Cavanagh, "Report of the Select Committee of the Brewers' Petition" (Cape of Good Hope, To Votes and Proceedings of Parliament, 1885), line 430.

Beer Excise Duty Bill (1883) brought in representatives of all of the local breweries as well as proprietors of local canteens, beer importers, and the Inspector of Excise, Thomas Crowe, to hear their objections or agreements to the bill. Fortunately for us, the ensuing discussions outlined the structure of the beer markets of the Cape Colony and showed that while every brewery produced pale ales, stouts, and export ales, the most important beer that they produced in the most bulk was tickey beer. Tickey beer was the cheapest and lightest of all of the beers that were produced by the brewers and made the most profit for most of them and due to the low cost, the primary consumers of tickey beer were Malays and poor whites.[65]

Cape Town brewers depended upon the sale of tickey beer. For instance, over the course of 1883, Anders Ohlsson's brewery produced five hogsheads of tickey to one of pale ale.[66] The head brewer and manager of the technical part of Cloete's brewery, R. V. Smith, said that they made thirty times more tickey beer than export ale and stout as well as about ten times more than pale ale or porter.[67]

According to Thomas Crowe, the Inspector of Excise, "tickey beer would compare with the low-class [running] ales in England."[68] He said this because they were both lower in alcohol, lighter in color, and had a short shelf life. They were also cheaper than other styles of beer and had a quick turnaround, which made them popular with consumers and brewers. Cape brewers agreed to an extent, but some argued that while the English beer corresponded in strength, the tickey beer was different by its condition due to the difference in climate that made bottling more difficult.[69] In Ohlsson's testimony against the passage

---

[65] Black South Africans were not a significant market for European style beer. They had their own local variety of beer production that did not impact the welfare of white South African brewers or beer importers. For more on the state of black South African liquor laws, consumption, and production, see: "The Report of the Liquor Laws Commission, 1889-90," with minutes of proceedings, minutes of evidence, and appendices, (Cape Town: W.A. Richards and Sons, Government Printers, Castle Street, 1890.)

[66] "Report of the Select Committee of the Beer Excise Duty Bill" (Cape of Good Hope, Appendix II, To Votes and Proceedings of Parliament, 1883), lines 209–11; or two-thirds to three-fourths of all production according to Anders Ohlsson, line 465.

[67] "Report of the Select Committee of the Beer Excise Duty Bill" (Cape of Good Hope, Appendix II, To Votes and Proceedings of Parliament, 1883), lines 279–80.

[68] "Report of the Select Committee of the Beer Excise Duty Bill" (Cape of Good Hope, Appendix II, To Votes and Proceedings of Parliament, 1883), lines 569.

[69] "Report of the Select Committee of the Beer Excise Duty Bill" (Cape of Good Hope, Appendix II, To Votes and Proceedings of Parliament, 1883), lines 65–6.

of the Beer Excise Duty Bill (1883), he noted that colonial brewers needed to have greater liberties than those accorded to the English brewers. This was due to the difficulties of the climate "because it is hotter and the fermentation is greater … We have to start very early in the mornings. At home, in the cold weather they can start at any time."[70] One of the key attributes of tickey that set it apart from the English running ales, according to David Thompson, the manager of the Letterstedt's brewery, was that it must be sent to customers "in an effervescing state. In England, [the clarity of beer] is all they care about, but here the Malays like it fizzing."[71]

In support of the increased beer duty, Thomas Crowe argued that higher prices would lead to better beer. The brewers, he argued, would have to recoup costs by using less malt and sugar, "making weaker beer which will be less intoxicating."[72] This would not alter the flavor, in his opinion. Crowe used Continental lagering methods as an example of how one could produce tasty low ABV beers in the Cape. He argued that "the brewer would not only produce a weaker beer but would take steps at once to store his beer and sent out a better finished article." Even though he was not a local brewer himself he attempted to convince the brewers that their beer "now sent into consumption is not a thoroughly finished article. To finish beer you must keep it in the store for six months" like the lagers of the Continent.[73] Crowe's description of a better beer mimics the metropolitan descriptions of Continental lager including its clarity, strength, and use of modern brewing techniques. Though he did not advocate directly for lager beer production, his descriptions and word choices were the same.

At the end of the committee's hearings, the Cape Parliament passed the Beer Excise Duty Bill (1883), which led to increased duties on both imported beers from Europe as well as locally produced beers. The most important and disastrous effect of the bill was the increase in price-per-bottle of tickey

---

[70] "Report of the Select Committee of the Beer Excise Duty Bill" (Cape of Good Hope, Appendix II, To Votes and Proceedings of Parliament, 1883), lines 407–08.

[71] "Report of the Select Committee of the Beer Excise Duty Bill" (Cape of Good Hope, Appendix II, To Votes and Proceedings of Parliament, 1883), line 308.

[72] Thomas Crowe, "Report of the Select Committee of the Beer Excise Duty Bill" (Cape of Good Hope, Appendix II, To Votes and Proceedings of Parliament, 1883), line 585.

[73] Thomas Crowe, "Report of the Select Committee of the Beer Excise Duty Bill" (Cape of Good Hope, Appendix II, To Votes and Proceedings of Parliament, 1883), line 588.

beer. Tickey beer went from its namesake 3p up to 4p. This price increase decimated the South African brewing industry, especially since a depression hit the colony at the same time. In 1885, South African brewers petitioned the Cape Parliament to rescind the excise duty so that they could affordably lower the price of tickey beer back to 3p.[74] Anders Ohlsson gave evidence for how impoverished the brewing industry had become by 1885 and according to his testimony, his brewery used to brew around thirty hogsheads of beer a day prior to the passage of the Act but with its passage, his brewery produced less than three hogsheads.[75]

The 1885 Brewers' Petition to the Cape Colony House of Assembly eventually led to the repeal of the Excise on Cape Colony-produced light beers, or those known as "tickey" beer. The Select Committee on the Brewers' Petition reached this decision after several weeks of interviews with beer importers, canteen owners, and representatives of several breweries around the Cape Colony. The Select Committee agreed that "a good business in the light beers is absolutely necessary to make the manufacture of the heavier or export ales pay" and that the "present Excise is inequitable, both to the brewers and to the consumers who prefer light beers to heavier drinks." All other duties, including those on imported foreign beer and any stronger beers would remain in effect.[76] This allowed the brewers to regain much of their tickey beer business with the return to 3p per bottle for their light, lower ABV, more carbonated ales.

The proceedings of the 1885 Brewers' Petition shed light on the state of beer consumption and production in South Africa up to 1885. The interviews lay out important information regarding the different beer markets, especially in Port Elizabeth and Cape Town. While the focus was primarily on the price of tickey beer, the prices of imported foreign beer, Cape beer of different styles, and the consumptive choices of different segments of the South African population were all covered. They show a reticence toward change and a loyalty to British brewing methods and styles of beer that mirror to those in the metropole.

---

[74] D. Cloete, J. Spence, and others, "Petition of the Undersigned Brewers Trading in Cape Town and the Vicinity" (Cape of Good Hope, 1885).

[75] Anders Ohlsson, "Report of the Select Committee of the Brewers' Petition" (Cape of Good Hope, To Votes and Proceedings of Parliament, 1885), line 182.

[76] Treasurer-General, Messrs. Wolf, Lewis, Theron, Dyer, Wood, and Fuller, "Report of the Select Committee of the Brewers' Petition" (Cape of Good Hope, To Votes and Proceedings of Parliament, 1885), xi–xii.

While they make reference to modern scientific approaches to brewing, the brewers themselves strongly supported their "practical" training via British methods. The most important beer style to Cape brewers was tickey beer, their own response to the growing trend toward light, low ABV beer that we saw in British running ales and Continental pilsner.

An important aspect of tickey beer, as argued by the colonial brewers, was that it was a necessary style to brew in order to make a profit because it was the most popular and best-selling beer they produced. Even though the Select Committee suggested that increased production of the stronger export ale would help to offset the loss of tickey beer consumption, the brewers argued that the "two must go together. There is not sufficient consumption of the better class [of beer] to keep the establishment going. The light beer is the principal thing."[77] This was because the first mash of the malt extracted most of the sugar, which was used in the production of stronger export ales. The later mashings of the malt would then extract whatever fermentable sugars were left in order to produce a much larger quantity of lower ABV tickey beer. Tickey beer allowed brewers to maximize economies of scale in their beer production and turn a much greater profit in comparison to their higher alcohol beer styles.

Cape brewers were not in competition with imported lager beers in the middle of the 1880s. The competition for beer consumers, as the 1885 Brewers' Petition highlighted, was between British imports and colonial brewers and not between colonial ale and German lagers. While the Cape brewers had control in Cape Town, they had stronger competition from English beer imports in Port Elizabeth.[78] Due to the Excise Act of 1883, Ohlsson's production of porter, pale ale, and export ale was in direct competition with English imports in Port Elizabeth "owing to the English beer being sold at the same rates [he charged] for all beers."[79] The breweries that they were in competition with were all from Great Britain and the metropolitan brewers had authorized their

---

[77] Anders Ohlsson, "Report of the Select Committee of the Brewers' Petition" (Cape of Good Hope, To Votes and Proceedings of Parliament, 1885), lines 187–8.

[78] Anders Ohlsson, "Report of the Select Committee of the Brewers' Petition" (Cape of Good Hope, To Votes and Proceedings of Parliament, 1885), lines 237–50.

[79] Anders Ohlsson, "Report of the Select Committee of the Brewers' Petition" (Cape of Good Hope, To Votes and Proceedings of Parliament, 1885), line 251.

agents to sell their beer cheaply rather than be cut out of the colonial market by competition with Cape beer. In 1885, this was working well.[80] Competition from Continental lagers, however, soon threatened the brewers of the Cape Colony and the British-style ales they produced.

Indeed, circumstances changed drastically in the next ten years. Joseph Chamberlain, the British Colonial Secretary, sent a dispatch to all of the British colonies at the end of November 1895 requesting information about the colonial markets.[81] The information returned from the South African Assistant Treasurer in July 1896 made it clear that the only beer imported into South Africa was from Germany. He explained that "it is cheaper and much lighter than the English, and the large German population in the Colony insist on drinking German brewed beer." Even though some English lagers had been put on the market, none of it was actually sold.[82]

As early as 1881, one-fourth of the beer imported into South Africa was German. By 1883, the imports from both countries were equal. Yet while the increase in German lager imports was great, it did not have much effect on most of the brewers in Cape Town. The reasoning given by one of Cape Town's beer importers, J. G. Steytler, was that "the people who drink German ales will drink Cape ale, for there is a great similarity. There are numbers of people who can afford to by English ales [but] drink Cape ales in preference."[83] However, there was one exception: the brewer of a short-lived lager brewery.

Adolf Krawehl worked at the Van Rhyn's brewery until disagreements with the owners over his management style in 1885 forced him to leave.[84] Prior to working for them, however, he had his own brewery that went bankrupt "mostly through the imported beer" brought into Cape Town.[85] Yet what was

---

[80] John Spence, "Report of the Select Committee of the Brewers' Petition" (Cape of Good Hope, To Votes and Proceedings of Parliament, 1885), line 304.

[81] Joseph Chamberlain, "Despatch to the Governors of Colonies on the Question of Trade with the United Kingdom," PRO DO 119/128/Misc. 103.

[82] Cape Town Chamber of Commerce, July 7, 1896, "Return Showing the Reasons Why Certain Articles Are Imported into This Colony from Foreign Countries, in Preference to Being Imported from Great Britain, No. 6 Beer and Ale" PRO DO 119/128.

[83] "Report of the Select Committee of the Beer Excise Duty Bill" (Cape of Good Hope, Appendix II, To Votes and Proceedings of Parliament, 1883), line 495.

[84] Adolf Krawehl, "Report of the Select Committee of the Brewers' Petition" (Cape of Good Hope, To Votes and Proceedings of Parliament, 1885), line 668.

[85] Adolf Krawehl, "Report of the Select Committee of the Brewers' Petition" (Cape of Good Hope, To Votes and Proceedings of Parliament, 1885), line 643.

unique about his brewery was that it was a lager brewery, the first and only one in South Africa until SAB began their own lager brewing in 1897. He said in 1885 that:

> when I started brewing, I started on the German style of brewing laager [sic] beer, with the use of ice. I bought a consignment of ice, about a ton, to the value of £5. When I had the brew ready, it was just at the time of the beginning of the importation of German laager beer, which my beer, on account of the low temperature at which it was brewed, fully equaled. It went to the Hansa Hotel, one of Cloete's houses, where the first imported laager beer went too, and it was imported in a large case, covered with sawdust. Of course, when I saw that I thought it would never pay to import beer like that, but afterwards they left the cases and simply imported in the cask. Then, of course, I could not compete … although at that time I had a brew ready of 300 gallons, which cost about £20. If it had not been for the imported beer, I should have been a well-to-do man to-day [sic].[86]

Years before South African Breweries, Ltd. began producing Castle Lager in Johannesburg, Krawehl had started the first lager brewery of South Africa. However, due to a lack of investment capital he was unable to exploit the potential economies of scale that Continental breweries used to keep their prices low.

Krawehl explained more about the process of lager brewing, showing the lack of knowledge about this style of beer by the Select Committee. He explained that it had to be brewed at a lower temperature than the Cape Colony ales produced by the other brewers and that the ABV was lower as well, aside from tickey beer. His pricing, however, would keep his beer far out of the reach of tickey beer consumers with a price of 6p. versus the sought-after return to 3p for tickey beer.[87] He argued for keeping all imports out of the Cape market so that he could start his lager brewery again without competition. When asked what would stop him from raising prices if he had no foreign competition, he replied that it was quantity that paid. His also clarified the difference between lager and Colonial ales.

---

[86] Adolf Krawehl, "Report of the Select Committee of the Brewers' Petition" (Cape of Good Hope, To Votes and Proceedings of Parliament, 1885), line 643.

[87] Adolf Krawehl, "Report of the Select Committee of the Brewers' Petition" (Cape of Good Hope, To Votes and Proceedings of Parliament, 1885), lines 647–8.

Krawehl explained that his German system of brewing did not need the tickey ale to pay for the higher ABV beers as the other brewers needed. His "way of brewing [was] different altogether [and he would] simply depend upon those who prefer better quality," intimating that his lagers were worth the much higher price compared to tickey beer and British ale styles.[88] Krawehl was an exception to the rule of British methods and beer styles in South Africa. Though he argued for the quality of lagers over Cape ales, he lacked the connections and investment that would have made his lager brewery successful in the early 1880s. Due to its low price the tickey beer, though similar in several respects to pilsner, remained the most popular style for the local populations of the colony. Once lagers were affordable with the establishment of South African Breweries and their Castle Lager, the British-style ales of the Cape, including tickey, could not compete.

In the middle of the 1890s, the Cape Town Chamber of Commerce was only interested in reporting beer and ale imports and the brewers of the Cape continued to focus on British brewing methods and beer styles. However, the recent founders of SAB quickly expanded their beer production to include lager beer in Johannesburg. One of the founders of the company, Frederick Mead, set to the task of organizing the necessary equipment for lager brewing in 1896. The Castle Brewery of SAB in Johannesburg soon acquired an entire lager beer plant from "the Pfaudler Vacuum Company of America who undertook not to supply their equipment to any other firm of brewers in South Africa and Castle Lager went on market in 1898."[89] The popularity of Castle lager was so great that all of the other breweries in South Africa followed suit and installed lager plants of their own.[90] Thus, the pilsner became the most popular style of beer in a British settler colony by the end of the nineteenth century as tastes went from British ales to tickey beers to the pilsner.

---

[88] Adolf Krawehl, "Report of the Select Committee of the Brewers' Petition" (Cape of Good Hope, To Votes and Proceedings of Parliament, 1885), lines 650–4.

[89] South African Breweries, LLC. Promotional Brochure (Johannesburg, South Africa, 1970).

[90] South African Breweries, LLC. Promotional Brochure (Johannesburg, South Africa, 1970).

Conclusion

The difference between the effects of tickey beer consumption in South Africa and the running ales of Great Britain was the influence of Continental migration and a lack of metropolitan nationalism that focused on specific beer styles. While the tickey beers were precursors to a transition to Continental-style pilsners in South Africa, the light running ales did not lead to widespread lager consumption in the UK due to the strong nationalist view of British ales in the face of Continental rivalries, especially with Germany, at the end of the nineteenth century and the early twentieth century. The British brewers lacked the motivation to retain control over colonial beer markets. Even their running ales that developed in response to changing tastes for lighter beer were produced for domestic consumption and not to compete with pilsner elsewhere. In comparison, there were many breweries in Bremen and Hamburg built for the purpose of producing beer solely for foreign markets. By the 1890s, there really wasn't much competition between the British and Continental brewers.

When British settlers in Johannesburg, South Africa began drinking and producing pilsner beer, they chose to identify more with the local multinational community than with the one they left behind in Great Britain. Beer and alcohol are unique forms of consumables, and very often the desire for community and intoxication can overcome those of loyalty or nationalism. This, in fact, was precisely what happened with pilsner beer in South Africa. Miners and other imbibers of pilsner were already sharing an experience of working together every day to earn a living in the gold mines of the Transvaal, and drinking alcohol together afterward was a natural consequence. With the most popular and cheapest beer being SAB lagers due to the economies of scale that the brewery was able to exploit, the miners chose to drink pilsner whether they were from Continental Europe or not.

This is similar to the lessons learned in the Cape Colony during the 1880s when tickey beer, the most popular and cheapest style of beer, became too expensive for most of the working population of the colony. This hurt the brewers enough that they called for the removal of the beer excise tax that had been put in place in 1883. Though Malays were the largest consumers, the working classes (like the Johannesburg miners) were the next largest group of tickey beer drinkers. When these groups could not afford tickey beer, the brewers suffered. When SAB lager arrived in Cape Town in the late 1890s, beer drinkers turned to pilsner—a better quality beer than tickey ever was—and forced Ohlssson's Cape Breweries to make lager as well in order to compete in the changing beer market.[91]

It was a combination of changing tastes, technologies, and investment that propelled the pilsner to its place as the global beer. South Africa is one example of the transition from British ales to Continental lagers but the vocabularies of taste may be used when looking at any national example where pilsner became the local style of beer. By following scientific and technological exchanges across imperial networks at the end of the nineteenth century we can also follow the changing tastes of European imperialists and local—and global—adoption of pilsner.

---

[91] "Ohlsson's New Lager Beer Brewery," *Brewers' Journal*, 8/15/1900, 457.

Conclusion

On October 10, 2016, the world's two largest brewing firms, AB InBev and SABMiller, merged to form a single company that controls nearly over one-third of the world's beer supply. The beers they are mostly known for are, no surprise, golden lagers, including America's Budweiser and South Africa's Castle Lager. It not only made them the largest brewing company in the world but one of the largest global companies in any industry. In addition to the multitude of breweries now owned by this multinational conglomerate, they also own numerous beverage and beer distribution companies, home brew supply companies, and much more. The scale of their vertical and horizontal ownership is astounding. As we have seen, the pilsner has come a long way since 1842.

This project has followed the rise and fall of the British brewing industry's dominance as the world's leading beer producer, followed by the rise of Continental European lager brewing. In the wake of the British ale domination, came the collaborative brewers with their golden lagers. Their brewing methods and beer styles spread across the world over the next sixty years and continue to have a place of influence in the twenty-first century both in the mergers of multinationals and in the hands of people barbecuing or playing games in their backyards or meeting in pubs or beer gardens the world over.

In the nineteenth century, none of this was a foregone conclusion. As the British held onto their national markets and traditional brewing methods, the Continental brewers sought to expand through the incorporation of companies and the adoption of scientific knowledge and technological innovation. By working together, Continental brewers were able to learn collectively and to carefully craft their breweries and brewing methods for efficiency. This collective learning, in turn, helped them spread their ideas, tastes, and products across the world. In comparison, British brewing languished as only British expats sought its inconsistent products in foreign ports and pubs.

The networks that developed out of European migrations and imperialism were key to the spread of pilsner and the associated industrial technology and production methods that came with it. Unlike most histories of migration and empire, this one goes beyond colony-metropole connections and includes extra-colonial players that had as much (and sometimes more) of an impact on colonial space as metropolitan players. South Africa's best-selling beer today remains the Castle Lager produced by AB InBev-SAB. Though the founders of South African Breweries, Ltd. were Englishmen, their methods and choice of product reflected the needs of the market and global connections outside of their nation of origin. The changing tastes of an interconnecting world at the end of the nineteenth century carried a single style of beer via imperial trade networks across nations and empires.

Over the following century, every former European colony, and indeed every other nation has developed a brewing industry that produces at least one golden lager, if not several. In many cases these lagers have become their nation's national brand of beer. What this means is that nearly all of the beer produced in the world derives from that original pilsner in 1842.

Tastes have recently begun to change as a result of the craft beer revolution that swept the United States in the last four or five decades. The craft beer movement began by setting itself up against the large industrial lager breweries. Beginning in the United States in the late 1960s and slowly spreading in the late 1970s and early 1980s, these brewers saw themselves as trying to find flavors that had been lost in their country. The golden, low alcohol, fizzy pilsners had spread so well that it was hard for anyone in the United States to find anything else. When several young American travelers took trips to Europe in the late 1970s and early 1980s they returned with a newfound taste for all of the different style of ales that had nearly disappeared from the Northwestern hemisphere.

The very attributes that made the pilsner the global style are the ones that many craft brewers were seeking to ignore and rebel against in their own beer. Dark, heavy porters, imperial stouts, sours, and super bitter double India Pale Ales are what many discerning craft beer drinkers seek. The rush to industrial uniformity that represented the modern progress of science and technology of the late nineteenth century pilsner brewers no longer holds appeal for the craft beer crowds that now stretch across many nations in the world today. Even one of the primary complaints about British ales in the late nineteenth century—that they were cloudy and had too much sediment—is now a sign of artisanal choice and status with hazy/New England-style IPAs.

Craft beer is the new wave across international borders. Unlike previous American cultural exports of commodification known as "Cocolonization" or "McDonaldization" that spread uniformity of flavor similar to the pilsner a hundred years before, this new cultural export is one of the choices of luxury artisanal beer. Brewers seek to push new flavors and use interesting, unique, and sometimes outright weird ingredients in the craft breweries that have been growing in areas as disparate as Ireland, South Africa, Italy, Central America, and across East Asia as well.

However, this "craft beer revolution" would never have occurred without something to rebel against. Without the work of the late-nineteenth-century lager brewers, the craft brewers of today would not be able to make beer as well as they do. For them it is a choice to make a sour beer or make it cloudy instead of clear. It is their choice to make their products different every time. This is because they use the scientific processes and technology developed by the pilsner brewers in Continental Europe, who spent decades working together to consistently make the same, consistent, stable, beer. Wherever people drink beer today and whatever kind of beer they drink there is a light, golden lager nearby, truly representing globalization in a glass.

Bibliography

Primary and Archival Sources

The National Archives (Kew, England):
CO 323/734/22
Do 119/128

National Brewing Library (Oxford Brooks University, Oxford, England)
Michael Jackson Collection:
Brock. *Dreihundert Jarhre Brauhaus Schwechat*. Wein: Selbst-verlag der Vereinigten Brauereien AG, 1932. Trans. Michael Jackson: MJ/4/17/45 Modern Sedlmayr Project I.
Scharl, Benno. *Beschreibung der Braunbier-Brauery im Koenigreiche Baiern*. Munich, 1814. Part V. Trans. Michael Jackson: MJ/4/17/45 Modern Sedlmayr Project I.

Guinness Storehouse and Archives (Dublin, Ireland):
Shand, Arthur. "Report: MR. Shand's Journey through South Africa." A. Guinness, Son & Co., Limited, St. James's Gate Brewery: Dublin, Ireland, 1904.

University of Cape Town (Cape Town, South Africa):
The Report of the Liquor Laws Commission, 1889–90, with minutes of proceedings, minutes of evidence, and appendices. Cape Town: W.A. Richards and Sons, Government Printers, Castle Street, 1890.
"Report of the Select Committee of the Beer Excise Duty Bill." Cape of Good Hope, Appendix II, To Votes and Proceedings of Parliament, 1883.
"Report of the Select Committee of the Brewers' Petition." Cape of Good Hope, To Votes and Proceedings of Parliament, 1885.

Published Materials:
100 Years of Brewing: A Complete History of the Progress Made in the Art, Science and Industry of Brewing in the World, Particularly during the Nineteenth Century. A Supplement to the *Western Brewer*. Chicago: H.S. Rich & Co., 1903.

Jalowetz, Eduard, Ivo Hlaváček, and Jindřiška Eliášková. *Pilsner Beer in the Light of Practice and Science*. Plzeň: Euroverlag, 2001.

Keeping Pace with the Nation We Serve: The Story of the First Seventy-five Years of the South African Breweries Group. South African Breweries, Limited: Johannesburg, South Africa, 1970.

Pilsner Urquell. Plzensky Prazdroj N.P. Plzen 1842–1982. Czechoslovakia, 1982.

South African Breweries, LLC. Promotional Brochure. Johannesburg, South Africa, 1970.

The Harvest of Our Soil: The Story of the South African and Rhodesian Breweries Group of Companies. The South African Breweries, Limited: Johannesburg, South Africa, 1961.

Correspondence:
Meiners, Leandro. "Empire in a Bottle," email, 2020, April 13, 2020.

Newspapers and Journals:
Allgemeine Brauer & Hopfen-Zeitung (1875–1914)
The Belize Advertiser, "The Beer Trade in Central America." December 29, 1888.
The Brewers' Journal (1864–1914)
The Country Brewer's Gazette (1877–8)
Times (London) (1787–1862)
The Times of India (1861–2010)

Secondary Sources

Adas, Michael. *Machines as the Measure of Men: Science, Technology, and Ideologies of Western Dominance*. Ithaca: Cornell University Press, 1989.

Auslander, Leora. *Taste and Power Furnishing Modern France*. Berkeley: University of California Press, 1996.

Bagnall, A. Gordon. "100 Years of Brewing in South Africa." In *The Story of Ohlssons*. Cape Town, South Africa: S.A. Hotel Reviews, Feb. 1953.

Ballantyne, Tony and Antoinette M. Burton. *Bodies in Contact : Rethinking Colonial Encounters in World History*. Durham, NC: Duke University Press, 2005.

Bauck, Sönke. "The Anti-Alcohol Movement in Argentina, Chile and Uruguay (ca.1870–1940)." PhD Dissertation, Forthcoming, ETH Zurich.

Beck, Roger B. *The History of South Africa*. Westport, CT: Greenwood Press, 2000.

Belasco, Warren James. *Food: The Key Concepts*. Oxford; New York: Berg, 2008.

Bourdieu, Pierre. *Distinction: A Social Critique of the Judgement of Taste*. Cambridge, MA: Harvard University Press, 1984.

Bulpin, Thomas Victor. *Tavern of the Sea: The Story of Cape Town, Robben Island, and the Cape Peninsula.* Cape Town, South Africa: Fish Eagle, 1995.

Bryceson, Deborah Fahy. *Alcohol in Africa: Mixing Business, Pleasure, and Politics.* Portsmouth, NH: Heinemann, 2002.

Cain, P. J. and A. G. Hopkins. *British Imperialism: Innovation and Expansion, 1688–1914.* London: Longman, 1993.

Chandler, Alfred and Takashi Hikino. *Scale and Scope: The Dynamics of Industrial Capitalism.* Cambridge, MA: Belknap Press, 1990.

Clancy-Smith, Julia Ann and Frances Gouda. *Domesticating the Empire: Race, Gender, and Family Life in French and Dutch Colonialism.* Charlottesville, VA: University Press of Virginia, 1998.

Cooper, Frederick and Ann Laura Stoler. *Tensions of Empire: Colonial Cultures in a Bourgeois World.* Berkeley, CA: University of California Press, 1997.

Crush, Jonathan and Charles H. Ambler, *Liquor and Labor in Southern Africa.* Athens; Pietermaritzburg: Ohio University Press; University of Natal Press, 1992.

du Plessis, Danielle. "The Brand that Stood the Test of Time." In *Marketing Mix,* Vol. 21 (7), 2011: 14–15.

Dumett, Raymond E. *Gentlemanly Capitalism and British Imperialism: The New Debate on Empire.* London: Longman, 1999.

Dyer, Peter. "'Pilsener Beer' in London in 1891." In *Brewery History*, (117), 2004: 36–9.

Ferguson, Priscilla Parkhurt. "The Senses of Taste." In AHR Forum in *The American Historical Review*, Vol. 116 (2), April 2011: 371.

Friedberg, Aaron L. *The Weary Titan: Britain and the Experience of Relative Decline, 1895–1905.* Princeton, NJ: Princeton University Press, 1988.

Gordon, Edward. *Sixty Years of Kenya Breweries.* Nairobi: Published by Dunford, Hall for Kenya Breweries, 1983.

Gordon, Robert. "Inside the Windhoek Lager: Liquor and Lust in Namibia." In *Drugs, Labor, and Colonial Expansion,* eds. William R. Jankowiak and Daniel Bradburd. Tucson, AZ: University of Arizona Press, 2003.

Gourvish, T. R. and R. G. Wilson. *The British Brewing Industry, 1830–1980.* New York: Cambridge University Press, 1994.

Gribbins, Keith. "The 40 Biggest Breweries in the World in 2021." *Craft Brewing Business,* June 13, 2022. https://www.craftbrewingbusiness.com/business-marketing/the-40-biggest-breweries-in-the-world-in-2021/.

Hall, Catherine. *Civilising Subjects: Metropole and Colony in the English Imagination 1830–1867.* Oxford: Blackwell Publishers, 2002.

Hennion, Antione. "Those Things That Hold Us Together: Taste and Sociology." In *Cultural Sociology*, Vol. 1 (1), 2007: 97–114.

Herring, Jonathan. *Intoxication and Society: Problematic Pleasures of Drugs and Alcohol*. Houndmills, Basingstoke, Hampshire: Palgrave Macmillan, 2013.

Ives, Martyn. *How Beer Saved the World*. Louisville, CO: Gaiam Americas, 2011.

Jones, David. "Top Four Brewers Account for Over Half of World's Beer." *Reuters*, February 10, 2010, accessed January 30, 2013. http://www.reuters.com/article/2010/02/08/beer-idUSLDE61723K20100208.

Kipling, Rudyard and Jan Montefiore. "Mrs. Bathurst." Explanation of Terms, In *The Man Who Would Be King: [Selected Stories of Rudyard Kipling]*. London: Penguin Books, 2011.

Kuparinen, Eero. *An African Alternative: Nordic Migration to South Africa, 1815–1914*. Helsinki: Finnish Historical Society, 1991.

La Hausse, Paul. *Brewers, Beerhalls, and Boycotts: A History of Liquor in South Africa*. Johannesburg: Ravan Press, 1988.

Law, Beatrice. *Papenboom in Newlands: Cradle of the Brewing Industry*. Cape Town, South Africa: B. Law, 2007.

McAllister, P. A. *Xhosa Beer Drinking Rituals: Power, Practice, and Performance in the South African Rural Periphery*. Durham, NC: Carolina Academic Press, 2006.

McCusker, John J. "Distilling and Its Implications for the Atlantic World of the 17th and 18th Centuries." In *Production, Marketing, and Consumption of Alcoholic Beverages Since the Late Middle Ages: Proceedings of the Tenth International Economic History Cong (Studies in Social and Economic History)*, eds. Erik Aerts, L. Cullen, and R. Wilson. Ithaca, NY: Cornell University Press, 1990.

McGovern, Patrick E. *Uncorking the Past: The Quest for Wine, Beer, and Other Alcoholic Beverages*. Berkeley: University of California Press, 2009.

Mager, Anne Kelk. "The First Decade of 'European Beer' in Apartheid South Africa: The State, the Brewers and the Drinking Public, 1962–72." In *The Journal of African History*, 40 (3), 1999: 367–88.

Mager, Anne Kelk. "'One Beer, One Goal, One Nation, One Soul': South African Breweries, Heritage, Masculinity and Nationalism 1960–1999." In *Past & Present*, 188, (188), 2005: 163–94.

Mager, Anne Kelk. "Trafficking in Liquor, Trafficking in Heritage: Beer Branding as Heritage in Post-apartheid South Africa." In *International Journal of Heritage Studies*, Vol. 12 (2), 2006: 159–75.

Mager, Anne Kelk. "Apartheid and Business: Competition, Monopoly and the Growth of the Malted Beer Industry in South Africa." In *Business History*, Vol. 50 (3), 2008: 272–90.

Mager, Anne Kelk. *Beer, Sociability, and Masculinity in South Africa*. Bloomington, IN: Indiana University Press, 2010.

Mathias, Peter. *The Brewing Industry in England, 1700–1830*. Cambridge, UK: Cambridge University Press, 1959.

Murmann, Johann Peter. *Knowledge and Competitive Advantage: The Coevolution of Firms, Technology, and National Institutions*. New York: Cambridge University Press, 2003.

Nagodawithana, Reedand. *Yeast Technology*. New York: Van Nostrand Reinhold, 1991.

Norton, Marcy. "Tasting Empire: Chocolate and the European Internalization of Mesoamerican Aesthetics." In *The American Historical Review*, Vol. 111 (3), 2006: 660–91.

Nurin, Tara. "AB InBev Announces Anticipated Close Date for SABMiller Purchase." *Forbes*, August 1, 2016, accessed August 5, 2016. http://www.forbes.com/sites/taranurin/2016/08/01/ab-inbev-announces-anticipated-close-date-for-sabmiller-purchase/#6d58944b4a02.

Nützenadel, Alexander and Frank Trentmann. *Food and Globalization: Consumption, Markets and Politics in the Modern World*. New York: Berg, 2008.

Oliver, Garrett. *The Oxford Companion to Beer*. New York: Oxford University Press, 2012.

Ogle, Maureen. *Ambitious Brew: The Story of American Beer*. New York: Harcourt, Inc., 2006.

Owen, Colin C. *The Greatest Brewery in the World: A History of Bass, Ratcliff & Gretton*. Chesterfield, UK: Derbyshire Record Society, 1992.

Parsons, T. G. "Science and the Victorian Brewing Industry, 1870–1900." In *Production, Marketing, and Consumption of Alcoholic Beverages since the Late Middle Ages: Session B-14: Proceedings, Tenth International Economic History Congress, Leuven, August 1990*, eds. International Economic History Congress, Erik Aerts L. M. Cullen, R. G. Wilson. Leuven, Belgium, 1990.

Pasteur, Louis. *Études Sur La Bière: Ses Maladies, Causes Qui Les Provoquent, Procédé Pour La Rendre Inaltérable; Avec Une Théorie Nouvelle De La Fermentation*. Paris: Gauthier-Villars, 1876.

Pilcher, Jeffrey M. "The Embodied Imagination in Recent Writings on Food History." In *The American Historical Review*, Vol. 121 (3), June 2016: 861–87.

Pilcher, Jeffrey M. "'Tastes Like Horse Piss': Asian Encounters with European Beer." In *Gastronomica: The Journal of Critical Food Studies*, Vol. 16 (1): 29–40.

Prestholdt, Jeremy. *Domesticating the World: African Consumerism and the Genealogies of Globalization*. Berkeley: University of California Press, 2008.

Purinton, Malcolm F. "Carlsberg." In *The Sage Encyclopedia of Alcohol: Social, Cultural, and Historical Perspectives*, ed. Scott C. Martin. Los Angeles, CA: Sage Publishing, 2015.

Rosenthal, Eric. *Tankards and Tradition*. Cape Town, SA: Citadel Press, 1961.

Sigsworth, E. M. "Science and the Brewing Industry, 1850–1900." In *The Economic History Review*, New Series, Vol. 17 (3), 1965: 536–50.

Streets-Salter, Heather. *Beyond Empire: Southeast Asia and the World during the Great War*. New York: Cambridge University Press, 2016.

Sumner, James. *Brewing Science, Technology, and Print, 1700–1880*. Pittsburgh, PA: University of Pittsburgh Press, 2013.

Swinnen, Johan F. M. *The Economics of Beer*. New York: Oxford University Press, 2011.

Teich, Mikuláš. *Bier, Wissenschaft und Wirtschaft in Deutschland 1800–1914: ein Beitrag zur deutschen Industrialisierungsgeschichte*. Wien: Böhlau, 2000.

Teich, Mikulas. "The Industrialization of Brewing in Germany (1800–1914)." In *Production, Marketing, and Consumption of Alcoholic Beverages since the Late Middle Ages: Session B-14: Proceedings, Tenth International Economic History Congress, Leuven, August 1990*, Aerts Erik Cullen L. M. Wilson R. G. International Economic History Congress. Leuven University Press, 1990.

Thompson, E. P. "Time, Work-Discipline, and Industrial Capitalism." In *Past & Present*, Vol. 38 (1), 1967: 56–97.

Topik, Steven and Allen Wells. "Commodity Chains in a Global Economy." In *A World Connecting*, ed. Emily S. Rosenberg. Cambridge, MA: Belknap Press of Harvard University Press, 2012, 593–814.

Topik, Steven and Allen Wells. *Global Markets Transformed, 1870–1945*. Cambridge, MA: The Belknap Press of Harvard University Press, 2014.

Trentmann, Frank. *Free Trade Nation: Commerce, Consumption, and Civil Society in Modern Britain*. Oxford; New York: Oxford University Press, 2008.

Unger, Richard. *A History of Brewing in Holland, 900–1900: Economy, Technology, and the State*. Leiden; Boston: Brill, 2001.

Unger, Richard W. *Beer in the Middle Ages and the Renaissance*. Philadelphia: University of Pennsylvania Press, 2004.

Walker, Cherryl, ed. *Women and Gender in Southern Africa to 1945*. Cape Town: D. Philip, 1990.

Walton, James. *The Josephine Mill and Its Owners: The Story of Milling and Brewing at the Cape of Good Hope*. Cape Town: Historical Society of Cape Town, 1978.

West, Michael O. "Liquor and Libido: 'Joint Drinking' and the Politics of Sexual Control in Colonial Zimbabwe, 1920s–1950s." In *Journal of Social History*, Vol. 30 (3), Spring, 1997: 645–67.

Wilson, R. G. and T. R. Gourvish. *The Dynamics of the International Brewing Industry since 1800*. New York: Routledge, 1998.

Wilson, Thomas M. *Drinking Cultures: Alcohol and Identity*. Oxford: Berg, 2005.

Wolcott, Harry F. *The African Beer Gardens of Bulawayo: Integrated Drinking in a Segregated Society*. Monographs of the Rutgers Center of Alcohol Studies, No. 10. New Brunswick, NJ: Publications Division, Rutgers Center of Alcohol Studies, 1974.

Index

ABV (alcohol-by-volume) percentage 6, 67, 140, 144–6, 150, 154–5, 157–9, 161–2
alcohol 3, 6, 34, 142–3, 154–6, 166
   low content 144–6
Allgameine Hopfen Zeitung 109
Allsopp's Pale Ale 131
Amaral, J. S. 111
American Civil War 102
ammonia-based ice machines 59
Anheuser-Busch Brewing Co. 136
Anheuser-Bush InBev (AB InBev) 1, 4
Argentina 111–12
artificial refrigeration 60, 62, 137
August Kruss 108
Australia 4, 10, 54, 89, 96, 101, 103, 121, 123–4, 131
   British colonization 133–8
   Continental beer 134
Australian Steam Lager Beer Brewery Company 135
Austria-Hungry, Nationalist revolts 101
Austrian Temperance Association (*Verein gegen Trunksucht*) 145
Automatic Generator 148

Balling, Carl Joseph Napoleon, *Die sacharometrische Probe* 41
Baltic Sea trade 33–4
Bass Brewery 152
Bavaria Joint Stock Brewery 44
beer production. *See also specific countries*
   basic description 15–17
   clarity *vs.* sediment 146–8
   consistency of taste 143
   industrialization 19–22
   low alcohol content 144–6
   nineteenth century trade 2–11
   quality 4, 143
   scientific methods 3
Berlin Conferences of 1884–5 114

Beschreibung der Braunbier-Brauery im Koenigreiche Baiern 36
Bieckert, Herr 111
Bieckert Brewing Company (Compania Cerveceria Bieckert, Ltd.) 112
biology 49–50, 63
Bismarck, Otto von 114
boiling 16, 21, 24, 49, 57–8, 105, 110
Bolivia 112–13
Börsch & Hahn Brewery 145
bottle washers 63
bottling 63, 89, 109–10, 142, 156
Brazil 108–11
   Brazilian Imperial Stout 110
   Brazilian Pale Ale 110
Brewers' Guardian 124
Brewers' Journal 1, 35, 62, 110, 139, 145–7, 151–4
Brewery Company, Bergedorf 44
brewing industry. *See also specific countries*
   beer production, basic description 15–17
   business tactics and domestic market 7, 13–14
   global trends and connections 1–2, 4
   industrialization 13, 19–22, 24, 30–1, 49
   Japanese 4
   national forms 128
   new technologies 3, 49
   quality 4, 22–4, 31–2
   scientific and technology 3, 24–9, 49, 64
   traditional methods 50
British ales 2, 4, 139–41, 148
   carbonation 148–9
   and Germany comparison 50
   lager *vs.* 17–19
British brewing industry. *See also* the United Kingdom (UK)
   from ales to lagers 124

Continental choice 30, 50
corporate espionage 32–3
export trade 33–6
forward-thinking breweries 64
funding 32
imports 35
investment and business strategies 14, 31–2
labor-saving mechanizations 29–30
lack of clarity 147
production methods 13–14, 22
publications 124
quality and quantity 13, 22–4, 31–2
science and technology 24–30, 49, 64
from 1750–1870 13–47
temperature control 57–8
trade networks 121–4
vertical design 23
British colonies 3–4, 6, 8, 10, 96, 120–4, 131, 134, 138, 160
British imperial trade networks
   geopolitics 121–2
   motivations 122–4
   non-German networks 121
   between rival nations 122
brown malts 29–30
Budweiser 4, 104, 165
Burton-Upon-Trent brewers 19–21, 30, 33–5, 38, 131–3

Cape Colony brewers 114, 140, 155, 158, 160–1
Caprivi, von 114
carbonation 11, 19, 67, 139, 141–3, 148–50
Carlsberg Brewery 37, 56, 61, 65, 69–70, 79–80, 99, 136, 144
Carlton Brewery 135
Castle Brewery 127, 162
Central America 107–8, 167
Cerveja Nacional 108
Chamberlain, Joseph 160
chemistry 50, 63
chemists 64
Citizens' Brewery (Burghers' Brewery) 42–3, 107
Cloete's brewery 156
Cohn, Julius 136
Cohn Bros.' Excelsior Lager Beer Factory 135–6

Continental beers 5, 17, 149, 151
Continental brewers 3, 5–8, 11, 13
   colonial markets 163
   consistency and palatability 71–2
   descriptions 141–2, 145–7, 149
   economies of scale 85
   from 1870–1914 123–8
   export markets 86, 91, 134
   funding 32
   German migration 99, 119, 121
   industrialization 19
   innovation 46
   knowledge and technology 39–40, 51, 76, 138, 165
   lagering process 147
   mashing methods 65–6
   motivations 101, 111, 118–19
   new business strategies 73–7, 82–6, 91–2
   overseas market 97
   professional programs 93
   quality and quantity 13, 95
   temperature control 57, 62
Continental pilsner beer 1, 67, 149, 159
   combination of elements 3
   export markets 4
cooling 17, 28, 39, 49, 56, 58, 60, 68
Copeland, William 118
corking 63
Country Brewers' Gazette 60
craft breweries 2, 4, 167
Crowe, Thomas 156
Cutler, Palmer and Co. 96

decoction method 65–6, 146–7
Dreher, Anton 38, 41–2, 45, 56, 148
   Kaiserbier 41–2
drying 39, 56

Ecuador 112–13
Engel & Wolf Brewing Co. 105
engineering 63, 89
English Industrial Revolution 21
ether, use of 59
Études sur la Bière (Studies on Beer) 64
Europe
   autocratic regimes 102
   Continental brewers 49
   export trade 50
   in nineteenth century 121

pilsner-style 13
temperance organizations 6
European revolutions of 1848 and 1849 101–2

Faulkner, Frank, *The Art of Brewing* 150
fermentation 17–18, 21, 24, 27, 39–43, 49, 99, 112, 126, 131, 157
   science and technology 50–1, 57–62, 64–70, 94, 136–7, 146–7, 154
First World War 102, 114–16, 133
food and drink, choices 139
Foster, Ralph 136
Foster, William 136
Foster Brewing Company 136–7
   Fermented and Distilled Drinks category 137
French cafés, London 151

German Beer Purity Law (*Reinheitsgebot*) 15
German brewing industry. *See also* pilsner beer
   business strategy 43–5
   cultural and culinary traditions 102
   export market 45–6
   industrial espionage 38–9
   industrialization 7
   lager techniques 36–7
   pilsner 36–7
   scientific and technological development 39–41, 49
   temperature control 58–9
   use of steam power 55–6
German migration 99, 119, 121
   motivations for 100–4
   North and South America 103–4
   pilsner 99–100, 102–4, 107, 112–13, 116–20
German nationalism 8–10
Germany. *See also* German brewing industry
   colonialism in Africa and Eastern Asia 113–17
   golden lagers 4
germ theory 2
Gladstone 27
Glass, C. G. 127
   Glass & Co. 127
glass bottles 63

globalization. *See also specific exports*
beer markets 2–3
pilsner 14
trading systems 6, 8
golden lagers 2–11, 122, 124, 140, 143–4, 146, 148, 150, 165–7. *See also* Continental brewers; German migration; lager brewing
   local consumption 4
Gold Rush 135
Gourvish, T. R. 7
Groll, Josef 42–3
Guayaquil Lager Beer Association 113

Hamburg Joint-Stock Company 111
Hansen, Emil 94
heat-exchange systems 28
Heineken 1, 62, 71
Heitmann, Koch, and Co. 113
Henry Pontifex & Sons of Albion Works 125
Hermann, George 113
Heuscheneider, Johann 116
How Beer Saved the World (documentary, Discovery Channel) 2
Huetteldorfer Brewery 42

Imperial and Royal Austro-Hungarian Consulate-General 46
India 4, 121
   alcoholic options 130
   Anglo-Indian elite 128–9
   British colonization 128–33
   malt liquor 131
India Pale Ales 2
industrialization 24, 30–1, 49
   beer brewing 19–22
Industrial Revolution 21, 24, 129
intoxication 141, 163
Ireland 4, 26, 35, 89, 108, 167

Jacobsen, J. C. 37, 56, 60–1, 70, 146
Japan 94, 99
   adoption of German lager brewing 117
   beer brewing industry 4, 87, 117–20, 138
   lager quality 133
Japan Brewery Co. Ltd 117–18
Jauche, Rudolph 116
Joseph Schlitz Brewing Co. 107

Kaiser Reich 119
King's Cross (London) 125
Kirin Brewery Company, Ltd 118
Krawehl, Adolf 160–2

labeling machines 46, 63
lager brewing 19, 36–7, 43, 53, 61–2, 93, 103, 107, 116–17, 134, 153, 161–2, 165
Letterstedt Mariendahl Brewery 126, 157
light ales 51, 140
Linde, Carl von 61–3, 111
Long, John 27

Mackinnon, John 132
Mackinnon & Co. 132
malting 15–16, 29–30, 49, 56–8, 69
    drying 56
maltsters 15–16, 38, 56
mashing process 16–17, 29, 65–6
    decoction method 65–6
    key methods 65–6
Mathias, Peter 7
Matienssen, Ernst 126
Mead, Frederick 127
Meakin, H. G. 132
mechanized refrigeration 49, 59–63
Merchandise Marks Act of 1887 46
Meux and Co. 60
microbiology 50
Mirwald, Vaclav 42
Moniteur de la Brasserie 62

Napoleonic Wars 33
Natal Brewery 127
Natanawa 118
National Brewery of Caracas 112
North America 4, 37, 101. *See also* United States
Norwegian ice 60

Ohlsson's brewery 125–6, 128, 156, 158–9
    continental scientific approach 126
O'Sullivan, Cornelius 30
Oxford Companion to Beer 2

Pabst Brewing Company 107
pale ales 2, 149–50

Paraguayan War 111
Pasteur, Louis 64
    Études sur la bière 26
pasteurization 68, 71–2
Payen, Anselme 39
Pedro, Don 108
Persoz, Jean-François 39
Pfaudler Vacuum Company, New York City 127
Pilsen Brewhouse 55–6
pilsner beer 3
    British beer comparison with 5
    business strategies 73, 76–7, 86–8, 91, 94, 97
    carbonation 148–9
    between 1870 and 1914 123–4
    key attributes 5, 14, 139–40, 144
    original light golden lager 8
    popularity 6–7, 147–8
    science and technology 51, 58, 67, 72
    sensory perceptions 141
    taste 139–42, 153–4
    trade networks 7
porters 2, 21–2, 24–5, 28, 31–4, 50, 58, 87, 92–3, 112, 115, 128, 134, 145, 149, 156, 158–60, 166
    industrialization 19–20
    pilsner comparison 14
    technical advantage 21, 31–2

quality 49–51, 66–8, 152, 156, 162, 164. *See also* taste experiences
    alcohol content 66
    Brazil 108
    continental brewing 24–7, 30–3, 35–7, 39, 71
    German breweries 87–8, 92, 95
    Japan 118, 133
    pilsner 42
    technology 52, 56–8, 143, 148

railroads 52–3
    refrigerated ice cars 61
Raw, George Henry 127
Reece's Patent Ice Company 59
Reinheitsgebot, tradition 118

Reutelshöfer, Georg Simon 107
Richter, Otto 113

SABMiller 1
saccharometers 21, 25–7, 39–41, 58
Saccharomyces Carlsbergensis (*S. pastorianus*) 70
Salt and Co. 131
Schwechat Brewery 38, 41–2, 56–7, 148
Schwechat Brewery Vienna 57
science and technology 5, 8, 24–30, 49, 63
   from 1870 and 1914 49
   fermentation 50–1, 57–9, 61–2, 64–70, 94, 136–7, 146–7, 154
scientific brewers
   golden lagers 50
   practical brewers *vs*. 63
Sedlmayr, Gabriel 37–9
shelf lives 49
Smith, W. Stanley 63
South Africa 4
   beer consumption 121, 140
   Brewers' Petition to the Cape Colony House of Assembly 158
   British colonization 125–8
   British methods. 158–9
   Excise Act of 1883 159
   Jan Martensz de Wacht 125
   lager beer 155–62
   Select Committee on the Beer Excise Duty Bill (1883) 155–7
   tickey beer 140, 155–6, 158–9, 161–4
South African Breweries (SAB) 127, 161, 164
South America 4, 107–8
Spaten Brewery 37–41, 43, 60, 62, 82
Squire, James 134
Standard newspaper 111
Statistical estimates of the materials of brewing (Richardson) 26
steam power 49
   economic and technical aspects 56
Steytler, J. G. 160
St. James's Gate Brewery 35
stouts 2, 51
Swakopmund Brauerei 116

taste experiences 139–41
   British traditions 153–4
   nineteenth century 142
   social context 141
Technical Association of Copenhagen 56
Technological Revolution 142
Teich, Mikuláš 7
temperature control 57–63
thermometer 21, 25, 27, 30, 32, 39–40, 57–8
Thomson, Thomas 27
Tickell, Henry 27
tied trade 31
Times (London) 131
transportation 49
   railroads 52–3
   steamships 53–4
   steam technology 51–2, 54
Triple Alliance of Argentina, Brazil, and Uruguay 111
Truth (British society journal) 153

The United Kingdom (UK). *See also* British brewing industry
   breweries 2
   colonial consumers 4
   exports 86, 89–92
   global trends 1–2
   industrialization of beer 19–20, 25, 35, 120
   lack of scientific education 147
   lagers 149–55
   porter style 14
   regional market 81–3
   technology 39, 92–3
   use of steam power 4–5
United States
   beer revolution 166
   breweries 2
   competitive advantage 74–5
   foreign-born population 102
   lager brewing 63, 104–7, 137
   local tradition 1–2
   pasteurization 68
   shipping revolution 54
   temperance organizations 6
Urquell brewery, Pilsen 127
Uruguay 112–13

Van Rhyn's brewery 160
Venezuela 112–13
ventilating machines 56
Vogel, M., 139

Western Brewer journal 110
Wilhelm I 114

Wilson, R. G. 7
Worms Brewing School 136
wort 26

yeast
    life cycle 64–5
    pure 51, 69–71

www.ingramcontent.com/pod-product-compliance
Lightning Source LLC
Chambersburg PA
CBHW052123300426
44116CB00010B/1775